maraca

VICTOR HERNÁNDEZ CRUZ

maraca

NEW & SELECTED POEMS
1966-2000

COFFEE HOUSE PRESS :: MINNEAPOLIS

COFFEE HOUSE PRESS is an independent nonprofit literary publisher supported in part by a grant provided by the Minnesota State Arts Board, through an appropriation by the Minnesota State Legislature and the National Endowment for the Arts. Support has also been provided by Athwin Foundation; the Buuck family Foundation; the Bush Foundation; Elmer L. & Eleanor J. Andersen Foundation; Honeywell Foundation; Lila Wallace-Reader's Digest Fund; McKnight Foundation; Patrick and Aimee Butler Family Foundation; The St. Paul Companies, Inc. Foundation; the law firm of Schwegman, Lundberg, Woessner & Kluth, P.A.; the Marshall Field's Project Imagine with support from the Target Foundation; Wells Fargo Foundation, Minnesota; West Group; and many individual donors. To you and our many readers across the country, we send our thanks for your continuing support.

Coffee House Press books are available to the trade through our primary distributor, Consortium Book Sales & Distribution, 1045 Westgate Drive, Saint Paul, MN 55114. For personal orders, catalogs, or other information, write to Coffee House Press, 27 North Fourth Street, Suite 400, Minneapolis, MN 55401.

LIBRARY OF CONGRESS CIP INFORMATION

Cruz, Victor Hernández, 1949–
Maraca : new and selected poems, 1965–2000 : poetry / by Victor
Hernandez Cruz.
p. cm.
ISBN 1-56689-066-7 (alk. paper)
1. Puerto Ricans—Poetry. 2. Hispanic Americans—Poetry. I.
Title.
PS3553.R8 M37 2001
811'.54--DC21
2001032479

10 9 8 7 6 5 4 3 2 1   FIRST EDITION
PRINTED IN THE UNITED STATES

Good books are brewing at coffeehousepress.org

Many of the poems in this collection previously appeared in the following books: *Papo Got His Gun,* a mimeographed book, was published in 1966; *Snaps* and *Mainland* were published by Random House in 1969 and 1973, respectively; *Tropicalization* was published by Reed, Cannon, & Johnson in 1976; *By Lingual Wholes* was published by Momo's Press in 1982; *Rhythm, Content & Flavor* was published by Arte Público Press in 1989; and *Red Beans* and *Panoramas* were published by Coffee House Press in 1991 and 1997, respectively. The poems in sections entitled *1966, 1967–1968, 1978-1990, 1993, Letters from the Island, Españole Caribe,* and *Seeds* have not previously appeared in book form. The author would like to thank the editors and publishers of the books listed above, and the magazines and journals where many of these poems first appeared.

To Ken Rosen
wherever you are
in deepest gratitude

CONTENTS

las maracas fueron los instrumentos que los behiques,
igual sus colegas del continente, usaban para invocar a
sus dioses. la palabra maraca, empero, es un préstamo
que les llego a los taínos de sus lejanas relaciones con los
guaraníes. en guaraní es voz compuesta de "maira" y
'aca':"cabeza de ser sobrenatural.

—NOTA DE JOSÉ JUAN ARROM

échale semilla a la
maraca pa'que suene

put seeds into the maraca so that
it could sound.

—AS SUNG BY CHEO FELICIANO

maraca

1966

Glow Flesh

you are falling
sun shine miracle
your lips are wet
                    rain
to our hearts
floods in every opening

on the stoop your skirt rises
fingers go up your legs

you are falling in the streets

the hallways of east harlem
the dark hallways of east harlem
the dark hallways with mattresses
of east harlem
                 you are falling
roll with us
the avenues
you are falling
the night
queen of the earth
you are falling
on us with lips
& thighs
& big round breasts
we hold in our hands
& hear your bomb tick
your blood get hot

come out
crack your eggs
on stupid american heads
queen of the earth
push us to the walls

fall on us
kill us
with your love
& tongue

harlem queen
fine mama
sprinkle us with it

there are no bargains
pure product
            you are falling

bloom bloom
you got all
sing

dark
& you shine
grown fat
for love

in the dark
you are like
a volcano
with a sea
of heat
        explode
        you are falling
        explode

A Poem for Downtown

(Some thoughts on a bus ride)

trees coming at you now
                    from the right side
trees only
            miles of trees
till now when we hit concrete
                            white walls
dead stone almost pressing against the window
the sun on the glass
making things look like paintings
clean gutters
look at the clean streets
run
bus go fast
the man is holding hands
because they are happy
                    they are not uptown
                    they are safe
                    so they think

but
on the side the stones are on the grass
& leaves are floating on water
                        everything is floating now
                        maybe even this bus

The Mystery

the neon signs
a line
up & down the Ave.
my feet have been
walking all night
into & out those ugly places/
          "Look man, look man, no light."
why have you been there
in the dark so long
sometimes alone
look here i am on this corner
those scenes in novels
are real funny
look how that lady walks
look how i have stayed up
all night
with the wind talking to me/

there was buildings remember
& they came to destroy them
made them into dirt/

a young girl said to me what do you want to do
with art—what have you done already—why are you
doing this to it—why

look how i plan
to wreck
made art into what comes out of
the streets.

look i remember those broken shapes
those trees around the corner
& cold hands on someone's throat
as if in another country

where are you today
in some basement
or on some roof
where even your touch
is alive.

Beyond Coney Islands

(Note: for some youthful 1966 reason I wrote this
poem in large caps . . . so I present it here as I wrote it.)

NO SWEETER THAN THIS

          A BRICK PASSING

                    I WONDER

I GOT TO LEAVE

      THIS PLACE

IS ANOTHER

     IS BIGGER & BETTER

IS BRIGHTER

      PASS WE ARE ONLY PASSING THRU

      THE WILDERNESS

      SO STRONG

         STRONG   KING SIZE & STRONG

TALL AS MOUNTAINS   BIG INDIANS

BIG INDIANS FROM THE ISLANDS   HUSKY & BRAVE

                INDIANS

KING SNAPS

KING SNAPS

    WONDERS

      THE HOUR OF DAY

      THE COLOR OF NIGHT

             UNCERTAIN

BE FOR REAL ALL

     LET THE LIGHT GO

     LET THAT SWIM IN THE STREETS

HOWEVER YOU WANT   WHENEVER YOU FEEL

& WHERE YOU WANT TO BEST

        SWING

      DRUMS & PIANO

      & TROMBONES

LIFT PAST THE CLOUDS.

from

papo got his gun

a mimeographed booklet published September 1966

The Land

for Albizu Campos

Our blue sea
now filled with cheap scum-bags
made in the USA
the continuous forests
now interrupted by Coca-Cola signs
the land something to buy
the yankee man touch everything
touch the sand
that saw Columbus
and our grass stepped on by Hush Puppies
the pueblo of my mother
of pretty music
of midnight songs
now sold in stocks
the yankee hand
touching my land
the touch of hate
the touch of death
Albizu locked in a cell
spoke of new times to come
I freeze in New York
a native of a hot land.

11:30 IN THE PARK

I stared for a long time
at her eyes
her big beautiful eyes
they were brown
her skin was brown
against the night
she looked dark
her lips were hard to find
but I found them in the dark night
her tongue was warm
her belly against mine
was round
and the noise of the river came to our ears
and we enjoyed it
the noise from the street came
and the noise from under the grass came
and the noise of the clouds came from above
and of the birds flying
of the ants eating
of the fish swimming
and all the time me and her kissing
in a while we left the noise
we left the night
we left.

Carmen

Why this girl has no fear
of night
Maybe she very wise
seen everything
has been there more than once
has seen the remains of the night before
has looked up at the moon from a crowded stoop
has seen the sun come out early
this girl is not afraid
seen the crowded street
seen the blood
everything trembling
she goes real smooth
she's been there
more than once.

1967-1968

The Music Is Like Search

for the Joe Cuba Sextet

What new word
that is soft like water
can i use for you
my love
and that burns like gasoline
to guide you into the night
what strange habits you have
the way you turn in a kiss
give it fire
torture it
till it screams
like a running whore
the hands are explorers
and the body the jungle
what will you find next
i know what it is
i know
how did you like Cookie
soft warm and sweating
what sound is that
whose side
sound like you lost something
the beat is the thing
even that sound will be my knife
you got a blade Victor
slice ass.

PIANO-PIANO-PIANO

for Eddie Palmieri

for all night
the grass at your fingers

walking with yellow thumbs
& drinking water
spread like a blanket
on the floor

wonder what he looks out to
if his fingers just touch
the piano goes on fire
       fast fingers

let tin cans get together
with animal skin
& produce a note
       we rise like fire
       like magic
       in the street
       a mile of noise
       heavy heads listen
       note
       going into space
       splitting molecules

piano-piano
       & let the door open
       he wants water
       got this thing
       red eyes
       in the almost
       dark room
       will turn killer

piano-piano
     making america
     as a floating chunk
     of garbage
     soon to go over
     the horizon
piano-piano.

FINAL POEM

1
The noise on the street
brown arms and brown heads whisper
wrinkled flesh
little bones—almost white
blood coming from where the head hit the gutter
crying in the back

like some mother lost her child
like some mother

Whispering—
                    a shout—a scream
an old lady's hand
going through the air on fire
like a shooting star
the screams go out of control—someone falls
an old lady's brown hands touch
the ground.

2
& then where the light wants to shine
someone gets in the way
& says: it is these buildings
getting high around you
you see lovely moon shining from the roof
puertorican trees
getting bright
Spanish-black town

getting dark
                    the black & puertorican moon
                    getting dark

& then where the light wants to shine
these things bother it

Out in the World

1
our heads leaned back to the lights
moving above
over the bridge
to the bronx
willis ave./179th street
under the el

back with claudia
tired & sleepy

to the el
paterson projects
3rd ave.
the bridge
125th street

out for carlos
down lexington
down third
112th street
off jefferson park

louie home

back on lexington
going uptown
light up some golden joints
to the bronx music palace.

2
let him kill that
drum if he wants to
go ahead
break it in half
make talk
make talk.

3
people fell asleep
heads against the table
musicians untie
themselves
walk on the stage & walk
off
all band jam session
people falling to the
floor
after 30 minutes.

4
squat by stage
heads leaning
touching the floor
eyes opening.

5
the sweaty necks
met the cold street
move fast
going back
cold train
our eyes close
darkness
& into the tunnel asleep

all the way
past your
stop.

The Story of the Zeros

zero
zero
zero

  the museum of modern art/is zero ugly cans
  & piles & piles that equal anglo zeros
  zero can O soup & O how wonderful the lady
  said about a geometric business machine
  zeroness is her/her empty zeros/the zero
  film the crowd made ape sounds & vomited
  their chairs/as they spoke later about how
  some zero would equal some other zero/also
  other's zeroness compared with another zero
  ness/it was zeros talking zeros/& about other
  zeros doing zero things/around zeros/things
  that came from computer & IBM/zero said to
  zero what about his latest film O it's
  really his best do you not think/O & she was
  such a good actress/hehehehahhhah rowa ro wa
  rawarearaaaaawaaaraaaratraooooo/the zeros
  walk from can to can from zero to zero to
  zero within zero/in the zero building of zeros
  & some zeros try to become $\frac{1}{2}$ but they are
  the biggest zeros/within zero books/some zero
  said they going to write book on zero culture/
  the amount of zeroness in the modern novel/or
  do development of zeroism in poetry/or zero
  play/& how zeros went to puerto rico & tried
  to add up/& how zeros went to são paulo &
  tried to do the samba/how they went to nairobi
  & tried to give some rice/& to/da nang searching
  for weird things to get into/but all them zeros
  did was to become bigger zeros & uselessness
  & de museum started raining dollars & all de
  zeros tried to get one.

BORICUAS & BLACKS

ly
from west to east
side
uptown music
thru the park
thru the chants
thru the windows
thru the indian
girl's legs
we spoke spanish
in the parks
boricua night time
time boricua
boricua/boricua
soul sisters
& soul brothers
boricuas & soul brothers
together
ly from west
to east
in dances not
recorded/in harmony
rice & beans
chitterling
greens & cuchifritos
elements of rhythm
drums/spirits/animal
skin/elecua/shango
obatala/espiritu
indio-
ly

from west to east

ly
ly
ly
ly
ly
ly
ly
ly   & you'll see.

from

snaps

1969

White Powder 1

in the dark corners of buildings
where politicians & their gray men
won't be caught dead
                    are the new arms
smacking themselves heads
                        the chinese
eyes/the red spots of the eyes/have
stories/lean back on piss-dried mattress
open up or melt at the corner
                        the nails
run thru the body scratching out need
now run up/smooth
                    burn the shit some
more he said/it ain't ready
                        who said when
the city sleeps/pass the last project/
exchange a deck/bars full of secrets/eyes
follow pool balls/almost falling to the
ground
        in the dark corners
        where brothers wait the hours
walking up & down with sweet soda/wiping
sweat/water spilling/
                    the trey bags are
so empty/tongues lick the paper/slowly
moving/
            but missing the light
            missing the light
            & there is so much to see
                            like
gringos & their gray men laughing.

Today Is a Day of Great Joy

when they stop poems
in the mail   & clap
their hands & dance to
them
when women become pregnant
by the side of poems
the strongest sounds   making
the river go along

it is a great day

as poems fall down to
movie crowds   in restaurants
in bars

when poems start to
knock down walls   to
choke politicians
when poems scream &
begin to break the air

that is the time of
true poets   that is
the time of greatness

a true poet   aiming
poems   & watching things
fall to the ground

it is a great day.

Snag

1
i thought of you
early morning
my eyes still not open
your eyes leaning against the wall
& the beautymark behind your knee

(but i'm making this up; am i)

the way you threw your arms
into my coat
& yelled it's too big
but did not matter

anyway
it's early morning

2
who are they over there
singing in a corner
beer cans in hands
passing Luchow's
not looking in to see their boss
or to smell the food

early Sunday mornings
i do things like this
or i think of something better.

Going Uptown to Visit Miriam

on the train
old ladies playing football
going for empty seats

very funny persons

the train riders
                  are silly people
                  i am a train rider

but no one knows where i am
going to take this train

to take this train
to take this train

the ladies   read popular
paperbacks   because they
are popular   they get off
at 42 to change for the
westside line   or off
59 for the department store

the train pulls in & out
the white walls   dark-
ness   white walls   dark-
ness

ladies looking up   i wonder
where they going
the dentist   pick up
husband pick up wife
pick up kids
pick up grass?
to library   to museum
to laundromat   to school

but no one knows where i am
going to take this train

to take this train

to visit miriam
to visit miriam

& to kiss her
on the cheek
& hope i don't
see sonia on the
street

But no one knows where i'm taking
this train
        taking this train
        to visit Miriam.

CITIES

> (moved singing/laughing/feeling/
> talking/dancing)

1
subway in
subway out
grove street
nine blocks
fifth ward
downtown
jersey city
the avenue
empty & lit
the store owners
hanging out
the doors
making legal
robberies.

2
we trust
the stairs
of a building
& they are
not even ours.

3
new projects
elevators
highways
snow
pot & hashish
stereo music
pucho & the latin
soul brothers
disturb
anglo-saxon

middle-class
loving
americans.

4
washington st.
the kind of party
you have to take
your hanky out
a bag of smoke
with a nail
inside
i mean/shit
i've seen a whole
lot of shit pass
for grass
but a nail.

5
together
drag your feet
in the snow
it's new year's
they say.

6
the kidney foundation
wants more money
& if you eat cheerios
you'll have power
so says the TV
that woke me up.

7
central
dance-hall
musicians
smoke before
they come out
the red exit

sign
the blue lights
girls with
black leather
pants
sweet
talk
&
sweat.

8
little cousins
play on your
fingers & head
& want kisses
before you leave.

9
they had women
in their pockets
a story of the
harbor
clowns came to town
hollering
they kick they ass

shit like that.

LATIN & SOUL

for Joe Bataan

I
some waves
            a wave of now
                        a trombone speaking to you
a piano is trying to break a molecule
is trying to lift the stage into orbit
around the red spotlights

a shadow
the shadows   of dancers
dancers   they are dancing   falling
out that space   made for dancing

they should dance
on the tables   they should
dance inside of their drinks
they should dance on the
ceiling they should dance / dance

thru universes
leaning-moving
            we are traveling

where are we going
if we only knew

with this rhythm   with
this banging   with   fire
with this   all   this   O
my god i wonder   where are
we going
            sink into a room full of laughter
            full of happiness   full of life
            those dancers
            the dancers

are clapping their hands
stomping their feet

hold back them tears
                                all those sentimental stories
cooked uptown   if you can   hold it for after

we are going
                away-away-away
                beyond these wooden tables
                beyond these red lights
                beyond these rugs & paper
                walls beyond way past
                i mean way past them clouds
                over the buildings   over the
                rivers   over towns   over cities
                like on rails   but faster   like
                a train   but smoother
                away past stars
                bursting with drums.

2

a sudden misunderstanding
                                a cloud
                                full of grayness
a body thru a store window
                                a hand reaching
                                into the back
                                                pocket
a scream
          a piano is talking to you
          thru all this
          why don't you answer it.

Born to Be Burned

1
it was no dream
it kissed you
& you flew away
with your head
on fire.

2
the same radio
plays
two years
fifteen times to the
floor
clothes
& wood

&
TVS
&
beds
&
baby carriages
&
chairs
&
the river
on the
picture
on the
wall.

3
it was slow spring
just coming by
no dream
screams
easter screams

asking god to come
his head
first hit the
garbage can
it fell hard
from the sixth floor
it bounced
& smashed into
the tar
he did not move
the god he called
did not come
thru the flames/

MEGALOPOLIS

(megalopolis—is urban sprawl—as from
Boston to NYC, Philly, Washington,
D.C., the cities run into each other)

highway of blood/volkswagens crushed up
against trees
it's a nice highway, ain't it, man
colorful/it'll take you there
will get there round eight with corns on
your ass   from sitting
turn the radio on & listen/   no
turn the shit off
let those lights & trees & rocks
talk/going by/go by   just sit
back/we/we go into towns/   sailing the
east coast/westside drive   far-off
buildings look like castles/the kind
dracula flies out of/new england of houses
& fresh butter/you are leaving the nice
section now   no more woods/into rundown
overpopulated areas, low income/concrete walls
of america/a poet trying to start riots/
arrested with bombs in pockets/conspiracy
to destroy america/america/united states/
such a simple thing/lawrence welk-reader's
digest ladies news big hairstyles with all
that spray to hold it/billboards of the high-
way are singing lies/& as we sail we under-
stand things better/the night of the buildings
we overhead flying by/singing magic words
of our ancestors.

THE EYE
UPTOWN & DOWNTOWN
(three days)

1
good things always happen
for instance
cats jump from building
to building in silence.

2
the dope on the
corner moves slowly
junkies dance the
boogaloo.

3
sleeper's head
is crushed against
the concrete
blood stains his ears.

4
one dice weighs
more than the other
knifes went thru space.

5
who knew
who stole
their bullshit
from their lips.

6
the long line
turns
slowly moves
inside.

7
buildings talk spanish
at night.

8

she had everything
she hated.

9

people walk the wall
they let them walk
the water
do the concrete pull.

10

his things are
wherever he wants them
to be
into any street
full.

11

the soft summer wind
has the smell of the
building on the corner.

12

junkies rob their mothers.

13

CURA CURA CURA
BAILA BOOGALOO.

14

watch the clothes burn
& wonder who put it on fire.

15

let the sun
send all it
wants
& we love it.

16

the piano lost its
teeth
the trombone fell apart
the conga drifted.

17

madison is good way
downtown
& way uptown
fuck the middle.

18

the lexington train
broke down.

19

a parade
of smokes
didn't get far.

20

everyone falls asleep
the radio plays memories
glass falls to the floor
the window left open
the lights make shapes
the rooftops hold hands.

21

trees get in the way
of dumb ladies sticking
out of windows.

22

everyday you turn
& turn again
it gets brighter
peep-peep-peep.

23

the stairs are full of holes
one big hole
no stairs.

24

stop sending the
wire downtown
stop talking
& do the rough ride.

25
BANG BANG.

26
small talk
turns into
gutter stomp.

27
the garbage truck
rolled over his ears.

28
what time is the
lame session over.

29
hospitals full with death
pigs
& lonely nurses.

30
death everywhere
coat cut
throat slit
smash against a wall
blood
wallet three feet away
empty.

31
the stories came
this happened
in this manner
which ever
ways.

32
slow the city up
watch
let it all hang out.

/ MOVING /

> mambo con conga
> is Mozambique/
>
> *for Eddie Palmieri*

la caliente   or how would we all
                        talk   if lips are
                        left to us   after
                        an hour or even a minute
                        after

mozab-mozab
          after a second
                        he fell back
                        covered with sweat
                        leaning
                        leaning   to a kind
                        of time   to a
                        splashes   & we
                        don't know   not yet

of all those new bags
unopen bags
          que suene la conga ahora
          que suene la conga ahora

mam
mam
     we don't know
                not yet

of all   all those   waves
we fell the nerve   the nerves
all of them   but we don't know
yet
   till some-some
          thing
                comes   running   out
                                             out

under lights   all   ways
under all the lights
all ways   to sweating
off   off to a start
                    on any
                         talkers

any   trying to
              run

& it follows   screams
brings   takes
furious   & destroying/
                    finish   right

fin-
   (& arawaks fly thru the air
   to protect   being   the only
   to save   watch out stepping
                         now

watch out   softness   to the lights
like forever   Could   this   air
Could last forever/
                    watch   spots
                    shadows up now
                    shadows   to the
                    floor   outside
                    is   falling   with
                    beats flying stepping
& arawaks like bebops)
                    in stone
                         stoned

how would you talk/sound/dance
in stone

a comer
a comer

todos a comer
       para   que
       para
       para que
       todas las veces
                 comer

te lo   & forever   some
                    thing

tho   we know not yet
not yet
      shadows   left behind

& mozab   mozab   mozambique,
                  thru the veins
                  & mozambique
                  thru the veins

to the heart   the heart/&
                    after
after   in the world
              cold
fearful   & dry & wet
               on the earth
all ways
     of
      the ways
ah   ah   the way
thru space
       not sure

a la la la la la
  con tego   lalala
          con te ga lala
si echo pa'lante
que suene
      (& arawaks be bebops
      bops the arawaks
      bebopping   arawaks;
      be bebops)

44

& he leaned
to the lights
& sweat
       & magic
tho   we understand
                it came
                     wondering

dancing up & down the walls
up & down the walls
like suave people
real suave dancer/people
mam——MAM***
mam   mom
          a sky without the blue
          or blackness   a sky
          only a sky
          he stood   arms in the
          air   in front
forever
    & we don't know
    & we don't know

       yet

be the drums/drumming your own death
be they/drumming your own death

mozambique   forever   ever
mozambique/
       listen
      moving standing
       standing unfinish
       a new wave

       for ever
       moving/at the Village Gate/victor

everybody passed the drummer/drummers in the park
drummers in the sky/

               we went up six flights
               looking down at garages
               & stores & listening to
               drums/all the way from
               the park/all the way from
               the sky

everybody
staring out/riding the roofs/look at the lights
of palisades/the round circles in the black sky
float all the way to the edge of the park/standing
by the river   the blue lights & red lights of
commerce/the windows of brooklyn/

               monk dropped his glass
               on someone's head/cause
               that's what he wanted to
               do/all over a shirt/& what
               about it

everybody
hanging on like clothes on the line/drummers
writing poems in the sky/drummers pulling off
their shirts/the trees echo the passages/& we on
the roof quietly resting/looking at summer/at
the lights that the city creates/the airplanes
shoot by over highways   & rivers/

everybody
passed by the drummers/roofs & windows over
head & eyes on fire

from

mainland

1973

A veces, de sus roncos altamares ocultos, de esas inexploradas distancias, vienen ecos tan vagos, que se pierden como ondas desmayadas sobre una playa inmóvil de bruma y de silencio. Son mensajes que llegan desesperadamente del ignorado fondo de estos dramas secretos: gritos de auxilio, voces de socorro, gemidos, cual de un navío enorme que naufraga a lo lejos.

Sometimes, from its hidden hoarse-voiced high sea, from those unexplored distances, come echoes so vague that they lose themselves like swooning waves on an immobile coast of mists and silence. They are messages that reach us in desperation from the unknown depths of these secret dramas; cries for help, voices, moans like those from a huge ship that is being wrecked in the distance.

—Luis Palés Matos

#3 BUSINESS

Don Arturo says:
There was a man
who sold puppets and whistles
for a living
He also played guitar
He used to go
to the shopping areas
and draw huge crowds
They bought his whistles
and puppets
They threw money into
his guitar
This was against the law
So he was arrested at
least three times a week
When his turn came up
in the courtroom
He took a puppet out
and put a show on
All the detectives
and court clerks
rolled on the floor
When he finished
they all bought puppets
and whistles from him
The judge got angry
and yelled:
What kind of business
is this
And the man said
I am the monkey man
and the
Monkey man sells
Monkey business.

Thursday

Water is Manhattan
The trains and the buses they sail
Stores and the lights
In the water wet
Thursday far and near strange
A dream Thursday and island
There are two in the memory

What forces elevated me today
To look for what I need
This corner of this earth
Searching for a way to know you
Venus
Thursday Jupiter
Land of somebody's fathers

Wet lines between us all
As the city is bombarded by rain
Young as you are
Young as I am   young as the world
Young History

Now we open doors
Now we remember continents and how they
Danced under the water
Under the ground

Was it Thursday
Was it Thursday
Let me look at you Thursday
Let me look all inside your secret
Open your arms
Elevate
Like rising music
Like that music
That I love so much

Like that Spanish that you like to talk
Like the way you walk

I hold Thursday all in my arms
In the deep tunnel I hear your hair
As it brushes against your neck
As you move
As a dance
Coming to see what it is all about

I build bridges in the sky
Send waves of thoughts
Do you hear them?

Today I eat guineo
With my hands
Under a palm tree by the beach
Where I am not
Do you see the dance that could begin
Evolve.

Los New Yorks

In the news that sails through the air
Like the shaking seeds of maracas
I find you out

Suena

You don't have to move here
Just stand on the corner
Everything will pass you by
Like a merry-go-round the red
Bricks will swing past your eyes
They will melt
So   old
Will move out by themselves

Suena

I present you the tall skyscrapers
As merely huge palm trees with lights

Suena

The roaring of the trains is a fast
Guaguanco
Dance of the ages

Suena

Snow falls
Coconut chips galore
Take the train to Caguas
And the bus is only ten cents
To Aguas Buenas

Suena

A tropical wave settled here
And it is pulling the sun
With a rope
No one knows what to do

Suena

I am going home now
I am settled there with my fruits
Everything tastes good today
Even the ones that are grown here
Taste like they're from outer space
Walk y Suena
Do it strange
Los New Yorks.

DISCOVERY

Watching a thousand smiles
that were full of sadness
standing in a wall
all sideways
My ears are the walls
No one can see me there
I am quiet
Still
Like the owls who sit atop
telephone poles

The traffic between
the walls
Those smiles that come
and go
Those darkened whiskers
suspended in the air
Those souls
Spirits
Coming from one thing
and going to another
but belonging nowhere

The walls breathe
My ears are hung like
blankets
My legs disappear into the
roof
My hands touch the building
next door
I swing from the walls
to the ceilings
No one hears me

I watch a yellow dress
that floats across
the rooms and stares
out of the windows

The Saints walk through
the walls
San Martin has a whole bowl
of grapes sitting on
the altar
he eats one every time
he walks by

Words come out of the rooms
like millions of fire crackers
They slam
Dance against the walls

On a clear Jupiter
The sun enters
Works its way in
Through the parted curtains
It moves inside the yellow
dress that hangs on
Yolanda

So
If you see a yellow dress
flying
Looking down on those
who walk the earth
with borrowed shoes
It's only Yolanda
cooking food
In through the door
and out through
the roof

My ears are the walls
And they hear it all
The yellow dress
It sometimes slips
and falls
Way in there
Where a smile
is six hundred miles
Way in there
where the Indians went to/

BERKELEY/OVER

1

Bird wings over the bay
Electronic bombs below
Waves talking to la moon
A town of philosophical habits
Cold turkey would kill it
So it just sits and cops
Everyday.

2

An empire of hidden houses
Behind the green wall of the hills
Staring down into the flats
Eyes looking for the airport
Where are the birds?

3

In the University a parade of sounds
Light show Music and Gowns
Talking walking
One day
When the sun came after the rain
Burgundy Almadén
A bit for San Pedro
The rest for the music.

4

The place had grown many
Creators from across the land
Some sit high up on the sides
Of hills
Others walk miles just to visit.

5

When the Monsoon came
And some found nothing to do
But stare at candles
The house on Grove Street
Was the secret meeting place
For those who wanted to hear
The rhythms
Pure.

Part Four

on 22nd and folsom
pacific ocean fish   boiling
far away and getting farther
a mean ice breeze sneaks upon
the city   makes everyone
speed up
when there is nothing to do
and the walls of the top floor
half a house no longer can
hold an urge to fly somewhere
and when lips have been pressed
together for three nights
walking around   studying hills
and wondering what 3,000 miles
away is like   after turning
down folsom of this west coast
city   head for the bay
looking for some loud beings
to show on the screen
at the edge of the nation
counting back on the population
and rows of homes   asleep
standing on the   last breath
of the town action
the moon   she comes down
and spreads her
legs wide.

CALIFORNIA #2

In the hour of Fresno
A strong blue
Yellow god
Valley of no rain
Afternoon walks
Full of wind from the
tips of the hills

Gypsy sings a song
And we walk toward
the car
And travel to the secret
two-room dwelling
To laugh and sleep
on the floor

The Hispanic morning
of Aztlan
Welcomed with Café
con Canela.

THE SOUNDS OF COLORS

for Joe Overstreet

painting #1
Go into
stars/the bluest
night in the world
the message loud & clear
red on purple
loud people of the
streets
turning into walls
as Chinese rockets
explode.

painting #2
Brown & blue waves
of nature
floating ladies
laughing gringo boredom
above
butterflies that throw
bombs and Missiles
happy holiday
on canvas bright.

painting #3
By the window
the owl sits in
yellow awareness
Filled with blackness
& love.

painting #4
The aztec sun
is warm
round eyes that
sparkle
quiet lips
deeply behind a painted
face.

painting #5
Purple orange blue
yellow walls
shooting shapes of
other worlds
geometric moons/spin
around its mysterious
creator.

INTERSTATE 80

Boola got off
in Salt Lake City
to sink down to
the town of Spanish Fork
and look for a treasure
left by a cousin of
Montezuma way
back when Columbus
knelt in front of
Isabel and sobbed
tears all over
her toenails

M.R. Fitz was heading
for Boston
and her long skinny
legs spread and
photographed the
driver/he wanted a
side pose

a gentleman fell off his
strong two feet his
1956 Fabian wig flew
to the side

From Oakland to Chicago
Brian O'Toole a Mayflower
special citizen/hit the
bus toilet 87 times
we counted

Three pairs of sunglasses
from Reno to Omaha were
melted by el Sol/the
teacher of the moon & the Ocean

Olando S.
saw an ancestor of his in
some Mountains in
Colorado and got off
the bus.   I am sorry
but he was overwhelmed
and could not be stopped
he said he would contact you
after the eclipse

An old brother man
he spoke about losing
his teeth near San
Diego in a fight with
a gringo who tried to
stop him from entering
he never went back
he spoke of a woman
he slept on every night
she is there/y mi hija
también.

I'm from Denver
she said . . . soy buena
con la gente/my children
will grow into the sky
and shine again

mira/rainbow dance
baila/tu rainbow line
line all shades/mira rain-
bow line to mexico/to mexico
rainbow line . . . dance baila
y dice/dance baila y dice
en el sky rainbow line
point and see . . . mira rain-
bow colores en el cielo
mira rainbow colores en el cielo
dancing up ahead . . . mira bailando
como es/seven colors pass your

head/mira rainbow dance/bus
follows clouds on top
of rainbow dance/mira así es
miro así es . . . rainbow dance
to México from ice up north
to México/el rainbow dance
seven colors chasing each
other cross the land air
mira baila con the rainbow
walk on the red/to México
walk on the red to México
walk on the red to Jalisco
and dance/mira baila con eso
que bueno esta/in seven colors
the rainbow ahead/put your
eyes in the blue mirror of
sunglasses and the window
will disappear/produce a
vision as long as days.

Nebraska

La luna
Sang the miles por los palos
de Nebraska
You bunch of lights
And houses   How did you walk
to this place
Buffalo Bill
Better know him some Spanish
Para Horses   ride
rubber horseshoes
moderno.

El café
Boiled water/no milk in sight.
Homes that will travel interstate
80 tomorrow in the morning
for the next edge of town.

The cowgirls/the local rodeo
As they galloped by their hair
unmoved by 15 miles per hour wind
It seems that 25 pounds of hair spray
is enough to hold a mountain down
Their hair style longer than their
faces.
Que Pasa?
Y los palos
do not feel at home any more
La luna
goes round the star dotted cielo
Let's watch
In this part of Mexico
Se habla inglish.

AFRICAN THINGS

o the wonder man   rides his space ship/
                                        brings his power through
many moons
                carries in soft blood   african spirits
dance & sing in my mother's house. in my cousin's house.
black as night can be/   what was Puerto Rican all about.
                                                all about the
indios & you better believe it the african things
                                        black & shiny
grandmother speak to me & tell me of african things
                                        how do latin
boo-ga-loo sound   like you
                        conga drums in the islands   you know
the traveling through many moons
                        dance & tell me black african things
i know you know.

—

Loíza Aldea

to José Fuentes

Loíza
Who is there   in you took
a walk   Sandy walks
y José y Jane   in Loíza
the rain
The Coconut that had wings
of rum
In that bar-café   Sunday
night
Palm trees are the first
to wake in the mornings
and walk around the streets
Loíza—who was you

"who that in deep natural
woods . . . who that walking
naked in the forest rain
who that . . . if it's as sweet
as the dulce de coco then
come here we would like to
eat"
She came when she came in
dreams
When she came
Above her Flamboyant red feathers
She hears laughter and song
She hears all the salsa that
is played on her ground
They hit six drums with one hand
She knows all the Aldea
Lit up with la Fiesta de
Santiago   Lit up like natural
glow from the mangos hanging
from the trees
Horses dressed with gowns

Coconut faces parading
Mediania Baja
Tumba/un quinto from the night
If legs played drums
The body moves like the drum
Drum/in motion tumba   The song
jumps on the head—the head jumps
like the leg/sounds like the
drum   drum talk to body   tumba
Body talk for drum
fingers make it laugh   Body
come so close   Loíza   is the
wind you like to blow
Above the town your legs
unfold   Everywhere you
look carnaval   a sea of laughter
dancing   coming
The plaza is full
In brown sandals we walk
the walks   we stand to eat the
food   shirts are opened
Breeze Loíza you are soft and
warm
The waves
The red dresses
The pink and yellow
La plaza la plaza lit
The Merry go round the smell
of shuffling bodies
Loíza
Loíza Aldea
On fire
Over there where fruits dance
into your mouth
& love comes gently
We sit till the morning
The wind blows festive sleep
Loíza you are always there
Silent with your African swing
Salsasa.

The Man Who Came to the Last Floor

There was a Puerto Rican man who
came to New York
He came with a whole shopping bag
full of seeds strange to the big
city
He came and it was morning
and though many people thought the
sun was out this man wondered:
"Where is it"
"Y el sol donde esta" he asked
himself
He went to one of the neighborhoods
and searched for an apartment
He found one in the large somewhere
of New York
with a window overlooking a busy avenue
It was the kind of somewhere that is
usually elevatorless
Somewhere near wall/less
stairless
But this man enjoyed the wide space
of the room with the window that
overlooked the avenue
There was plenty of space
looking out of the window
There is a direct path to heaven
he thought
A wideness in front of the living
room
It was the sixth floor so he lived
on top of everybody in the building
The last floor of the mountain
He took to staring out of his sixth
floor window
He was a familiar sight every day
From his window he saw legs that
walked all day

Short and skinny fat legs
Legs that belonged to many people
Legs that walk embraced with nylon socks
Legs that ride bareback
Legs that were swifter than others
Legs that were always hiding
Legs that always had to turn around
and look at the horizon
Legs that were just legs against
the gray of the cement
People with no legs
He saw everything hanging out
from his room
Big city anywhere and his smile
was as wide as the space in front of him

One day his dreams were invaded by spirits
People just saw him change
Change the way rice changes when it is
sitting on top of fire
All kinds of things started to happen
at the top of the mountain
Apartamento number 3 2
All kinds of smells started to come out
of apartamento number 3 2
All kinds of visitors started to come
to apartamento number 3 2
Wild looking ladies showed up
with large earrings and bracelets
that jingled throughout the hallways
The neighborhood became rich in legend
One could write an encyclopedia if one
collected the rumors
But nothing bothered this man who was
on top of everybody's heads
He woke one day and put the shopping bag
full of seeds that he brought from the island
near the window
He said "para que aproveche el fresco"
So that it can enjoy the fresh air

He left it there for a day
Taking air
Fresh air
Gray air
Wet air
The avenue air
The blue legs air
The teenagers who walked below
Their air
With their black hats with the red
bandana around them full of cocaine
That air
The heroin in the young girls that
moved slowly toward their local
high school
All the air from the outside
The shopping bag stood by the window
inhaling
Police air
Bus air
Car wind
Gringo air
Big mountain city air anywhere
That day this man from Puerto Rico
had his three radios on at the same time
Music coming from anywhere
Each station was different
Music from anywhere everywhere

The following day the famous
outline of the man's head once again showed
up on the sixth floor window
This day he fell into song
and his head was in motion
No one recalls exactly at what point
in the song he started flinging the
seeds of tropical fruits down to
the earth
Down to the avenue of somewhere big
city

But no one knew what he was doing
So all the folks just smiled
"El hombre esta bien loco, algo le
cogio la cabeza"
The man is really crazy
something has taken his head
He began to throw out the last of the
Mango seeds
A policeman was walking down the avenue
and all of a sudden took off his hat
A mango seed landed nicely into his
curly hair
It somehow sailed into the man's
scalp
Deep into the grease of his curls
No one saw it
And the policeman didn't feel it
He put his hat on and walked away
The man from Puerto Rico
was singing another pretty song
His eyes were closed and his head waved.

Two weeks later the policeman felt
a bump coming out of his head
"Holy shit" he woke up telling his wife
one day
"this bump is getting so big I can't
put my hat on my head"
He took a day off and went to see his
doctor about his growing bump
The doctor looked at it and said
it'll go away
The bump didn't go away
It went toward the sky
getting bigger each day
It began to take hold of his whole head
Every time he tried to comb his hair
all his hair would fall to the comb
One morning when the sun was really hot
his wife noticed a green leaf sticking

out from the tip of his bump
Another month passed and more and more
leaves started to show on this man's head
The highest leaf was now two feet above
his forehead
Surely he was going crazy he thought
He could not go to work with a mango
tree growing out of his head
It soon got to be five feet tall
and beautifully green
He had to sleep in the living room
His bedroom could no longer contain him
Weeks later a young mango showed up
hanging from a newly formed branch
"Now look at this" he told his wife
He had to drink a lot of water or he'd
get severe headaches
The more water he drank the bigger
the mango tree flourished over his head
The people of the somewhere city heard
about it in the evening news and there was
a line of thousands ringed around his
home
They all wanted to see the man who
had an exotic mango tree growing from
his skull
And there was nothing that could be done.

Everyone was surprised when they
saw the man who lived at the top of
the mountain come down with his shopping
bag and all his luggage
He told a few of his friends that
he was going back to Puerto Rico
When they asked him why he was going back
He told them that he didn't remember
ever leaving
He said that his wife and children
were there waiting for him
The other day he noticed that he was

not on his island he said
almost singing
He danced toward the famous corner
and waved down a taxi
"El Aire port" he said
He was going to the clouds
To the island
At the airport he picked up a newspaper
and was reading an article about a mango
tree
At least that's what he could make out of
the English
Que cosa he said   Wao
Why write about a mango tree
There're so many of them
and they are everywhere
They taste goooooood
Como eh.

from

tropicalization

1976

Cada Loco con su tema

——POPULAR SAYING

from New York Potpourri

Side 1

Me go in plane traffic
drinking Cola-Champagne la original
Floating
everytime I come to giant city
Hear tambores
inside of New Yorks flying
big legs
Yellow taxis flying glowing
through all streets
Where Con Edison beating the ground
Eternal repairs
Orange lights
Blue lights
Green lights
They should dig dig dig
All the way down
till they hear the voice
Of their mama.

Side 13

Horses and roosters are parading
down 5th Avenue in celebration of
Wednesdays when you wake up in the
mornings and wonder what they will
Bring
shoot me underground
Way cross town
Good days
Bad days
Each day a thought
Turns into movement
Pops visible on the corners
dressed in things and singing
Leather coats hot like the sun

Tickets at half price
Everyday horses and roosters
wake me
and they want to sell me something
that belongs to nobody.

Side 27

So many windows have lost
their power to hold back the wind
Millions of bricks getting tired
And sick beyond medicine
Dragging to the next decade
Marine Tiger who didn't eat
Millions of hands
Shirts and blouses
Nostrils how many
Shoes millions
How many little buttons in New
York
Little dimes in little corners
How many notebooks and pencils
How many wheels and pictures
Hanging on tanto walls
Sideways y upside down
Left ways alley ways right ways
Do you know the 7 deadly sins
Back ways or front ways
Choo Choo loco motives for all
this population holocaust
STOP
Disappearing and melting
Appearing vanishing
My body dressed in orange
In purple blues and turquoise
Wake up all the pirates
and their women
La danza of words tonight
The only thing that can hold truth
Among these ten trillion windows
of light.

Side 32

I am glad that I am not one of those
Big Con Edison pipes that sits by the
River crying smoke
I am glad that I am not the doorknob
Of a police car patrolling the Lower
East Side
How cool I am not a subway token
That has been lost and is sitting
Quietly and lonely by the edge of
A building on 47th Street
I am nothing and no one
I am the possibility of everything
I am a man in this crazy city
I am a door and a glass of water
I am a guitar string cutting through the
Smog
Vibrating and bringing morning
My head is a butterfly
Over the traffic jams.

The Latest Latin Dance Craze

First
You throw your head back twice
Jump out onto the floor like a
Kangaroo
Circle the floor once
Doing fast scissor work with your
Legs
Next
Dash towards the door
Walking in a double cha cha cha
Open the door and glide down
The stairs like a swan
Hit the street
Run at least ten blocks
Come back in through the same
Door
Doing a mambo-minuet
Being careful that you don't fall
And break your head on that one
You have just completed your first
Step.

ENTRO

He says nada
Yo digo something
Happenin cuando el calendario no marka
las notas de los días y dayś como querids
que saesd—Fue también una complication
de sitio—tú sabes-de to espacio aya en la
mente de la gente—que díos nunca te ponga
en sus bocas—O vocas de vocational—vacacíones
enteras pasaron y el calendario se rompió-fué
tú sabes———que ni él que era él y él me de you
tú sabes-aquél día que me encontré contigo
y tú empiesas—pueh él dijó nada-y and aquello
también Yo digo que sí—que si se pueh ablar
de lo que uno a visto—por aiiiiiii pa ya- por
to eso de donde somos-son y seran de donde
estamos—tranquilos y locos—perturbados por
la pertución—de lo que es—lo que es lo que es
todo eso anologos con jodisiqueviris–del top hassle
de esa sinofonía a tendro del hielo—sal de allí
compas-el New York Times mide las cosas con qué
Los leones escriben el alfabet con qué–él que
de quien tendra la verdad—cada coco en el invierno
sufre más por su linda visíon de-pero a todos los
comprendemos—su invierno sin calor—aquél que escribió
tan elegante paper—las palabras hacien fuá-por su
calor por su colores el sabor de su calor-colorids
tenía en la grammar conoció todo el glamour
El tuvó su gran por qué—pero estaba-está-equivocado-
también se le complico la cosa a traves los oids-
tú sabes-tú sabes él no supo en que se hablaba—pueh
vio cosa que yo no vi-tú sabes—appeariención-pués se
entiende que el Brain lo están estudiando todavía-So,
quiere decir que la cosa sigue-porqué el centro de lo
central que se discute aquí quien puede decir lo
que es con estos rayos electricos informativos que contro-
lation public sabor de que-device que siembran en tú
espacio—hay que penetrar directly keep going anyway

por que-y to los días que la oscuridad nos mira-pasamos-
pasan por encima-días y noches no markados por el
calendario—que Ay bendito ehta OUT OF ORDER/atendro
de esta cosa que contiene todo para los especialistas
de estructures y criticos a caballo-y sober y crackiow
historians—y que lástima la maquina se rompió.

Three Songs from the 50s

Song 1

Julito used to shine the soul
of his shoes before he left for
the Palladium to take the wax
off the floor while Tito Rodriguez
flew around the walls like a
parakeet choking maracas
It was around this time that
Julito threw away his cape
because the Umbrella Man and the
Dragons put the heat on all the
Ricans who used to fly around
in Dracula capes swinging canes
or carrying umbrellas
Even if there was no rain
on the horizon
That same epoca my mother
got the urge to paint the
living room pink and buy a
new mirror with flamingoes
elegantly on the right hand
corner because the one we had
was broken from the time that
Carlos tried to put some respect
Into Julito and knock the
party out of him.

Song 2

All the old Chevies that the
gringoes from upstate New York
wore out
Were sailing around the neighborhood
with dices and San Martin de Porres
el negrito who turned catholic
Hanging in the front windows.

Song 3

There was still no central heating
in the tenements
We thought that the cold was
the oldest thing on the planet earth
We used to think about my Uncle Listo
Who never left his hometown
We'd picture him sitting around
cooling himself with a fan
In that imaginary place
called Puerto Rico.

1978-1990

UNTITLED

You have pretty legs
and Ponce de Leon hidden in your closet
like a birthday gift from the old world
he stands right next to your flowered bikini
panties
Adorned in his garb of madman
bad taste under the sky of Rio Piedras

So you keep your indian locked in a box
he is too near you complain
to the mirrors which stare at your face
you want him to go away
You pull your long hair
the color of the coal
deposited in the basements
of the lower east side
the box is small like your hands
it keeps moving threatening your parties
and your friends who enjoy cuba libres

It is all so terrible Julia Maria
this sunny day between your legs
these talks of la literatura del pais
the quotes of los grandes poetas como Diego

I see that you go crazy this way
like someone in vast deep waters
who can swim the swim of fish
but would rather drown

It is impossible not to hear that
nation of West Africans you have locked
in the last room
You avoid the room like a mouse avoids
a cat

Today I saw you down by the beach
walking in circles with red bikini
falling off
Staring into the water
talking to yourself

Julia Maria you have Ponce de Leon
locked in your closet
And you have an indian in a box
and a nation of Africans in the last room

We stare out of the hotel balcony
the sun cooking all the people
It is getting late and you must go
to take those panties off of
Ponce de Leon's face

What is it that I hear down the street
the fiestas are coming soon
The sociologists are running home
It is only that what happens is not explained
if they explain they invent
A building falls to the right
they say it fell to the left

The sun turned into the moon
we turned corners outside
Until we no longer knew where we were
on the small island
"You know this place is small
but you can get lost."

[It is the Year 1125]

It is the year 1125
There is more to do in heaven than here
But wait I am inside of a guayaba tree
Waiting for a flight to the other side
You could have been picked up by a frog
That jumped off a rock
This was poetry
Ask basho
rock
frog
the other side
How do I know
The Pictograph on the rock
Poetry reading Poetry looking
One glance you are gone
What economy of words
Where are you now

The cohoba plant was the Taino peyote
It still grows wild in the mountains
Why don't we use it again
Instead of going to kmart
Instead of going to confession

Did our literature start with the letters of Columbus
Or were the pictographs the origin.
To be thrown on hammock reading leafs and vines
Waxing the beak of a parrot
Literature is the clear water of a river
A tall mountain where it rains God.

Dreams and Forms

Was it a room
or the moon
Or a mosque
in times so turban
Perhaps seashell
through the greenish
Train
if a locomotive
Shot out of el Yunque
was it Morroco or
1 04th street
near Lexington Ave.
Which had a subway
Entrance that you
could take to the
Museum
y Picasso walking *Guernica*
But what was this
church with shouts
Tambourine and timba
maraca holy spirit
Lips which spread
like cascabels
Are these walls or
carpets
Is this a room
or a mushroom
Fatima's golden hand
leads an orchestra
Like the ocean
Sara boats
Sirens from Spanish
Harlem where Rosa
Grows
midnight sucks eyes
Thrown against mountain
building

I saw what entered
the room
A tribe of men and women
in colors and jewels
That what ever was
tropical fish jumped
And the combination of
the birds
Some say Mohamet* appeared
Atlantic coast
Hand in hand
with Siboney
With a pipe so gold
red bricks float
Plaster of Paris prays
chocolate in milk dissolves
And once again I beg
is this a room
Or have I through
distance zoomed
Caribs squeezing through
lock
Make heads spin in orbit
bop
Merenque planet swift
shaking belly
Day night
night day
On and off
like someone messing with light
Switch
moon changes from slice
Of banana
to grapefruit
Through the window
I keep cool
While all around me
the warpath of the fool

* Peace be upon him

Jehovah slice the room
Agallu claiming the doors
I am trasluz when through
the door I introduce myself
With red pra-pra
I fix a glass of rum
When Altagracia taps me
with eyes celestial daze
That was for Caridad del Cobre
I am her agent on the
East side
I went to 305th heaven
Of only light for infinity
from there saw Sara
Walking gypsy heads
my eyes were looking
Out my feet
they took me down the stairs
As a rose Magdalena
passed
Her eyes so marble
as to roll out
Along with a song
being chased by
A horizon of drums
her hips and lips in
Roundness match
as through the winding
Stairs
a kiss I catch
It was then that I
felt my pillow
And my eyes came back
late for work
Back in capitalism
the embroidery of thieves.

[Do you need balcony fish]

Do you need balcony fish
and the rhythms of the ocean waves
Do you need walls with crosses on
them
White dresses waving in
salutation of the afternoon
Churches jumping hallelujah
Electric maracas radio
Maniacs of all colors
and features as if thrown at
random
Through a system of the
indioafroandaluz
Black hair JET
Breeze of Carib
Passion that concentrates
and jealous removes
While in its presence
Outside debris
Because this moment is nowhere
else
No ever else in the life of
banana being
Drag me out of bed rooster
6 in the morning
Reason or no reason
Need plaza and sandals
Marianetas
Toward fresh school
Monseratte corner
Fine stepping horse that
dances
With straw hat head
Rum drum tobacco mars
Pineapple brains upside down
Plate of mofongo
with sushi octopus

Mahogony legs of walking
sun
Melting cheese and preparing
wrinkles
As Doña Prana Umbrellas
Street toward mountain
Looking for the shade
The Caribbean is looking for the
shade
I even need occasional denque
and strange fever chills
Along with savage heat
God of caffeine bean
Staring from moutaintop
Demi taza of soft thigh bread
Need radio blasting
Clave

NÁ

It's always been always
now like then the same
Egypt is in the future
woman power decision
A man scrambles for reaction
his position imposition
Never has it been not been
always from from to from
Till the now and now
since cold thought it's winter
And bones fashioned meat
into designer bodies
And the two too is what
to be is
Even if within double one
saw sea
It wasn't first Matry and
then Patry
Given what was given
the sat and the had
Given that man invented
dance and singing
Appealing begging Saturday
to hatch
Watch musical wind makes
Colorado print in eyes
Fire patterns of sensuous delight
males carry the beautiful art
Outside
woman inside joy climb
Only turquoise steps leading
to purple orange carpets
With white pillows as if
clouds to bed
After singing blend
harmony and the story invented
By an aviator of the highest

flight
That only goes with that
to who stands and shines
The best drown the pest
isolated in thought the rest
The test of harshest laws
made with air that's bitch
The shadow of heaven
dissolves sons of whores
In light years of endless
nothing
Something had to pop
poppy seed
Papito
what else could it be
After all that traveling
through light and dark heavens
Metal heavens
cotton heavens
77 heavens of electrical static
Then heavens of perfect tonalities
of eternal maracas
Aeons of timbales
places from where the moon
Is the top of a conga
sending a tumbao into the
Ear beyond the planets known
where there is a wondrous other
Place that is coming back this
way
There is always something between
nothing toward something
That was the greatest thought
of eternal nothing staring at
Itself
holy shit it yelled
Lets turn the street and
send some fool to piss in the
Corner in a round shape room
stand still it is

And always look at always
that's what it was in the beginning
And forever tradition
of walking and dancing stars
Think of absolute originality
and even before that
And go ahead and drop dead
to experience the beauty that
Flies out of the echoes of
creation
Test it amidst the
overabundance of beautiful
Forms
pretty more pretty
Delicious more delight
guayava then mango
Maria then Sylvia
so it is that it had to be
And now that it is it is
what it is despite the is not
And the is so
is is
Go back easy to the forgotten
land
Nothing has happened here
everything stayed the way it
Was
nothing.
Ná

CARIBBEAN GLANCES

Magenta and then bronze
Purple and then cinnamon
Red and then red
White and then mahogany
Pink and then flamingo
Blue and then bolero
Yellow and then love
Green and then blue
Curve and then fragrance
Patchouli and then taste
Mystery and then caves
Wood and then a face
Eyes and then valley
Sorrow and then laughter
Beans and then water
Venus and then tobacco
Night Agua Florida
Morning and birds toward the rivers
Street and then straw hats
Christ and then everybody
Sunday everyday
Caribbean and then sky.

Is It Certain or Is It Not Certain
Caso Maravilla

> Note: In which two young independentistas
> are brutally beaten and killed
> by members of the intelligence division
> who claimed that they were on their way
> to sabotage a tower which controlled
> the electrical power for the San Juan
> area.

Cover up like mascara
Helena Rubenstein
Not even Paris in its glory
A man has to follow with a sack
To collect objects falling
Given that all objectivity has fallen
The backache is a confusion even
To the Chinese doctor

We're moving with legs down a hill of
what
Listening to a policeman present in the
jam
How he lost his memory
Remembered only that he had a coffee
Two witnesses down another officer
With an I didn't do it kind of face
Said
They had a trail of pork chops
Possibly some rice
And that everyone ate
And the previous police officer
who only recalled coffee
Had seconds according to this
witness
So much for digestion

We are walking up a hill
which is walking down us

Walk in front of Christ
carrying the cross
Pursued by maladies
Chasing the thoughts in your
Mucus head
This is the church people
Of decency repute
The bad people in this case
Are Satanás themselves
Mercy means the opposite
In the dictionary of the lard

Be careful
Cause look what is loose
And possessive of power

If a psychiatrist saw such fantasy
Him make for airport

Christians
Of the kind that sold themselves to Rome
Who maintain the language of the killers
Of Christ
As the ceremonial language of the very
Church of Christ

Condemn them
For they might know what they
are doing
And know no better

Police set them up like dinner table
For Queen Elizabeth
Every knife in its proper place
Saucers and plates at measured angles

Now that you have seen the beauty parlor
imagine the wig

Colonial Spanish language
was directional
Monolingual
A one way street
A question was also an answer
A mind which has nothing to give
Gives it vigorously
Force is what it has learned
From the monarchs
From the priest
Who made a generation of Tainos
transform into biology
to school teachers who teach
you the rules with the very rulers
The plan is to take over
what has been made
While you destroy those
who made it

They kill you one day
The next day they want to know
why you are dead
The Aztecs
The Romans
The armies
The police
Missionaries
who forever want to change beings
Obsessed with others doing something
wrong
This has created a knot
Which not even seven Houdinis
A place in which the devil
screams three times

The search light of the scrambled head
Veins where cheese travels
Watch tower eye head
Those who cannot live life will not
allow anyone else to live it
The plan is to put things in order

To balance the Libras
To put in place
To set straight
To cut to size
To sharpen up
To move out the way
To eliminate
To kill
To invade

Look what a small door
A bull is trying to push
Through dressed as justice
Caso Maravilla the tall
hill from which everyone must
Run
Senators
Judges
Governor
Desks
Police
Agents
Neckties
Microphones
Nails
Television
and all

Run into the
Rhythm of justice
Played by the drums of consciousness
Of original mountain rock

We know the proverb well:
You cannot cover the sky with your hands,
Especially if the sky is blood red

So be careful
and be cool
Even though
Caquax is hot.

Matterative

In late popular Latin madera is related to timber
and all its derivatives—now it doesn't matter in
specific it includes: stuff which a thing is made up
of—the sound of the word has been separated from the letters
matery-matiere-mate(e)re-matire-mater-mateer-mattir-matter
"As there is of poison to the spider where wuld be matter
of honi to the bee."—G. Harvey (1884). Within English,
you don't know how something looks like till you see it—Spanish
is specific to the rhythm of the sound—what you follow is that
timing for accuracy of letters—The sound of one language
given to the other is visual-audio translation—the kind of
reversal of gears for which a car has not been made yet. Shapely
of shapelessness what exactly is the form; where does this
matter now go—In Spanish matter is actual material and loses
the spaciness—since look there it is something: designated.
Matterative is substance with a motor. *Qué te pasa?*
Coming backward from the English: What is the matter: going
back to the Spanish—Qué te material: what have you produced.
Also what goes through you: raisins are also called pasas.
Singularly pasas passes. What occurs? There are more angles
than words—information not yet given a house a time of
piece/peace. The Spanish and English cross each other in
simultaneous tracks that are spelled different—though even
spellings can harmonize—the arrangement of reality tempera-
ment of each of the languages can be married within the spelling
system and framework of only one, either or—mono languagewise
not stereo or stereotyping: which means typing with two type-
writers at the same time.

> d. *In Kantian and subsequent use, applied to that*
> *element of knowledge that is supplied by sen-*
> *sation, regarded apart from the 'form' which it*
> *receives from the categories of understanding.*
> —*Oxford English Dictionary*

The night club is full of what matters to the spectacles
all sitting receiving and not getting—reception your full ear
here we go—to exactly:

> 1611—Bible, Acts XIX:38—If Demitrius, and the
> craftsmen . . . have a matter against any man, the
> law is open.

> —Oxford English Dictionary

Like who got the entire procession of beautiful words the whole
evening dancing—nothing that gave given—matter fills the tables.
Fried beans all over the California highway the mind is trying
to arrange itself as a coconut smoking tobacco: Nothing can
enter through either of the languages with similarity
of presencia. One moment you feel this, the next minuet
you see that. Latinamaniria native of the central avenue
where the sound tracks after the noise, these things all
have their differences, so one wave of a syllable comes
seconds after its necessity has been within a situation
acted out, it is like entering a cigar which is
made of the top of the mountains inside and the foothills
for a coat, pull that. Which way should it go is the
momento facility, vacant rooms in a motel; some orchestra
in the lobby: it decides which way itself, don't ask
another Why: Porque means because.
I wonder how that would be, something quickly dances buzzes
shows goes flows through the diameter of division, machine
pronosticaría, she still remains copper metal of pleasure
calm floating like a letter of the alphabet in New England
lake so hidden a hand caressing the graphs created by the
waves on a piece of paper.
Unworking things should have an immediate way of getting
out, keep trying, if not send it away, how many I's (eyes)
do you need. Beware of where like the period ends the
sentence, don't run off on to the next 2,000 years, fragments
remain and squat through another period, eternally someone
who is invented from the division is left behind in mirrors
and spurts of terror. Is all this condensation?
Separate the strong one she will laugh with you.
Wassamattar: Mat-ter, L. Materia, material, stuff wood.

Does the west side have more than the east side, any given
summer is not for free, who did it belong to that the language
does not express it, take something out—give it to me
immediately. What something is involved with is what it is
all made up of: "Tell me who you walk with and I will tell
you who you are" is an old saying of science. Constituent
substance: Con ti y tu: with you and me: what makes you
not me: constitución: with you and also with a song:
"Stange quark: An obligatory constituent of all strange
particles." Whatever is out there that has the ability to
be seen, what sits in space and waits for time to come. What
sits in trees, goes to parks and freeways, cities and
pretends; all that matters now matterized: that too is in there
deeply all the urbanites at the last of their juice: who
invented that number forever: Just a panorama—so something
is bigger than the things that come into it. What is inside
the manner of what he was not speaking about: As a matter
of fact the opposite of what is what? Something moving down
a street is itself the motion and spirit of the flesh, the
first thing to go, cemeteries for the archaeologist, dance
floor for the dancers, they both make themselves: equali-
zacíon. Significance is the moment, through aliven it
and expect it the same amount of size: forecast the weather
surprise will chacalaca right out of you. Who moo to
see Mouse in Alaska one time, pre-history animals—big and
over there: its age in the forest—what makes the avenues
the material for everything—taking transport—one death on top
of another or another is making all this: Overdoses, plastic
bags bodies of 14-year-old boys have left not understanding the
chemicals of nature: Too much heroin, not enough body: a high
pitch, Luisito's mother searches for definition, no one wants
to look at her eyes, her scream comes down from the window her
daughter embraces her. What's the matter, horseman, the music
stretches you out, there is no cocoa butter, they find you
calendars away. We don't interpret that from one place to another
the significance remains intact for all the days of sadness: no
overdose from too much guava paste: but the chemical was not
the problem, it is the connection; why we talk to what doesn't
listen: The material is very strong matter, matta is kill.

The Perfect Rose

We hear the town below sitting
through perfect stories of appearances
its initial arrival in an inward room
in the mountain forest you sign a contract
with the trees and they keep you in their
hideout
it begins after this glance to give more
details
hands touching you
throwing you off the bed or your name
jumping-in voice someone else's you don't
know how to see it.
scatter you fly with fear and piss your
next-to-last clean pants the color
of the night also wants you to obey
the stories they beckon
your hair on your arm vertical
but long ago we left your aunt
with her stories in the living room
from this afar we hear the collection
she got Mario in there and Fila
their eyes are on the walls
"how close was that woman
to her motherless daughter"
aha she came to this world to find her
in her loneliest moment
she looks just like the mother the
neighbors were sure that after her
husband killed her she came back about
all the beings constantly jumping out
of that house where a female scream
is an eternal reoccurrence
she is the only story that comes up
and discovers
where we had each other pinned up
you with a simple yellow dress,
that comes down below your knees

your hair held up by roses
my mustache one letter after the next
eating the pear-shaped tits in darkness
the whole town down below wondering
where we are
except the reincarnated whispers
they were staring right at us
but they do not trap not even their
forms
when there was another shift in the
tales
I ran out of my forehead
with all the stories of the mountain.

THE SOUND OF LOVE

San pronto no se wis windos cuan el calus de la
mañananana en el airsty es que tu desde po la me
cally fooly sa fo so mo to eh se onpeso a tocar
si yo ser nada su conjunto de alegría tal ves su
coro de la risa a mi me theo dan pati pami estos
communiqués dolores en el pecho parte atra parte
alounde y en ses lenguaje asi asi camina en el
verso tu pierna y tolla tu boca tis desde el primer
escalonosoco de dia tu puerta toca en mis labios
labytory de inversion tu cuerpo rompe la ventana
y hasta acaba con la pueh si ah.

FINANCIAL REPORT

No, no get plata free
Only lata gives here translated plains
Only the pains produced from seeing
And smelling clean leche must be
Sera the name of a woman see no
It is especulation if not it
Can be its opposite saying the
Same thing with a different jacket
Aqui no se vende dinero
When the snow is white in your
Ears humming you numb
They put fire to the lata
Flame to the can
Heat to the silver
Bend nickels
Actually sell you public opinion
And make centuality out of your
Fears
No have plata ni plaza ni neo Plaza
Where you have plasta of plata
Just a kind of lata which gets fevers
Plateforms Plataforms also don't
Cool the plate the flata la lata
Platanos   Plain things remembering
Two landwhichis.

The Cruelty of Love

The other day I remembered you
Very closely
You were coming from an epoca
That sits in the next room
The thought of a future species
Of flowers
Your eyes were like bolitas
Moons when they open wide
Machito's full arrangement
Of trumpets in "Ay Que Mate"
Is similar to your tickle
How much more mambo can we get
Missiles being launched from
Your eyes in waves
Jumping in and out
California sun melting you
Into some kind of vapor
A trail of steam is what
I remember
Now that I sing this song to you
Because you do it so well
And what of your name
When I stand correctly on the corner
I call you supreme butterfly
Sprinkle the air with:
Hi   a flor
Remember me in the coming
Springs of sadness
Where we construct our lies
In this life of cruelty.

LUNEQUISTICOS

In what language do you jump off one boat
to get to another one to buy something cold
to drink while at the same time you contemplate
The shapes and curves of the eyes the various
family trees have produced in all the people
present buying something cold to drink
The shades of minds each beaming glaze of their
spirit all being here for a second of my questions
I am in the young woman's tenor her lips drum
pictures of thin Spanish fans waving
Ships sailing in pictures hanging on living
room walls   Chaotic room of thirsty tongues
Moving my whistle sounds to investigate
Each glassy eyes my windows
Their fires in the cold drinks
So if I ask you my creature friends in what language
do I ask the question to come in: Do I take my
Oye/lo/que/one/time/eva/or/iva/decir/que/uno/una
ves/sepuso/la/cosa/de bullets/peor que/one guerra
en/the/escuela/corner/de/maestros/ya/con/lisencia
y/todo/una/mes/mass/de/masas/tambien/con/masa/cuando
ella/pasaba/lo/profesores/le/cantaban/siquere/gozar
ben/a/bailar/tengo/libros/de/to/colores/estudiaremos
el/at/most/fear/el/turn/de/una/language/como/hace/in
side/the/mind/calculate/while/it/separates/words/in/two
languages/sounds/spellings/systems/whole/tone/latitude
and/altitude/altiduego of voces/in/gas/communications/gets
filtered/and/ironed/tambien/the/two/musics/through/one/breath
Para/
    Or do I spray it around in straight talk
Filtar: Presuming you tailored the rough edges of your
tenor   dress it up with my wave of syllables say to me
What is your idea what flavor did you ask for
In what tense does it remain the same color when it
laughs in your cup.
Pure orange juice.
Pure ginger root-boiled.

Pure grapefruit—the ones with freckles.
Pure Spanish/Pure English
Pure tunes tos tono tos tones
When is exactly Saturday and Sabado two different nights
Do you say in one aspect of the night your deep feelings
to whoever might be involved in a need to hear them from
you or do you avoid what's really going on and talk other
heavens go over to the jukebox before ordering a cold
drink put on Tito Rodriquez's "Double Talk" put the boat
In reverse and relax you have just given birth to twins
The tongue figures out how not to jump from one boat to
another and takes a dash out onto the street where the
wrong speed can brake anybody's record.

Visibility 0

When the wind hits me at ten below
zero I talk to it about destination
the pensive street or streak inside
registering faster and faster
breathing is like snorting ice
this little jacket hanging on me
like fighting a lion with a razor
blade   I am being desecrated by
the wind which doesn't know me at
all doesn't know that someday I
will capture it and blow My own
whistle on its face
I try to enter my heart
by shrinking my shoulders toward
my chest
in some far-off place the wind
takes vitamins and comes back again
despite the blows I look at the
kids going to Junior High School
at the drawings on their loose-leaf
notebooks turquoise canvas with a
big heart in the middle a sword
running through it from top right
to left bottom the handle up top
from left top to right bottom a
lightning is shooting through it
in the middle of all this a cross
is emerging it in turn has bright
yellow rays jumping out
the heart inside is red and purple
I wonder now that all of that has
gone passed/past me if there was more
detail to be seen had it not been
ten below zero and mean
not even a thermometer could have
such a tale.

from

by lingual wholes

1982

The price a world language must be prepared to pay is submission
to many different kinds of use. The African writer should aim to use
English in a way that brings out his message best without altering
the language to the extent that its value as a medium of international
exchange will be lost. He should aim at fashioning out an English
which is at once universal and able to carry his peculiar experience.
I have in mind here the writer who has something new, something
different to say. The nondescript writer has little to tell us, anyway,
so he might as well tell it in conventional language and get it over
with. If I may use an extravagant simile, he is like a man offering a
small, nondescript routine sacrifice for which a chick, or less, will
do. A serious writer must look for an animal whose blood can
match the power of his offering.

> —CHINUA ACHEBE,
> *Morning Yet on Creation Day,* 1976

Now, as Reality is such as we have affirmed, know that thou art
imagination and that all thou perceivest and that thou doth designate
as "other than me" is imagination; for all existence is imagination in
imagination (that is to say "subjective" or microcosmic imagination
in an "objective" collective or macrocosmic imagination).

> —ABU BAKR MUHAMMED IBN AL ARABI,
> 1165-1240 AD

Vuestro lenguaje es muy incompleto para expresar lo que esta fuera
de vosotros; han sido necesarias comparaciones, y vosotros habeis
tomado por realidades esas imagenes y figuras. Pero a medida que el
hombre se ilustra, su pensamiento comprende las cosas que no
puede expresar su lenguaje.

> —ALLAN KARDEC,
> *El Libro de los Espiritus,* 1970

Anonymous

And if I lived in those olden times
With a funny name like Choicer or
Henry Howard, Earl of Surrey, what chimes!
I would spend my time in search of rhymes
Make sure the measurement termination surprise
In the court of kings snapping till woo sunrise
Plus always be using the words *alas* and *hath*
And not even knowing that that was my path
Just think on the Lower East Side of Manhattan
It would have been like living in satin
Alas! The projects hath not covered the river
Thou see-est vision to make thee quiver
Hath I been delivered to the "wildernesse"
So past
I would have been the last one in the
Dance to go
taking note the minute so slow
All admire my taste
Within thou *mambo* of much more haste.

ART-THIS

Lucy Comancho is an artist
Art this
She makes all the stars in Hollywould
seem like flashlights which have
been left turned on for a week
She had a *frenisi*
A friend in C
A friendinme
with paintings and blowing things
up into color which came from nowhere
No one knows where she got these things
Her mother says too much thinking
She painted the walls in her house
She painted the hallways and stairs
the stoops the garbage can tops the
squares in the sidewalk the tar on the
street the plastic bags from the cleaners
the brown grocery bags the inside of milk
containers   She herself had to be contained
from painting your face the closest layer
of the sky elements everything she gave
brush to rush to paint your *nalgas* if you
gave her room   She never thought of canvas
where they sell it absent from her view
Sometimes she was called Picassa feminizing
Picasso
She painted Josefina as I was writing
that Josefina is the feminine of José
Josés who are also known to go under the
nicknames of Cheos or Pepes and so
Josefina got tagged on her the name Pepa
which is female for Pepe and she dug that
Pepa for if you look close the other name
José *y fina* means José and thin or sounds
like *oficina* like Joseoffice also it had
something in it of José is *fina* José is
finis finished   no this for someone being

composed by an artist
To top it off Pepa also means *pit*
you see what is inside of fruits   This
is all in Spanish and something is being
lost in the translation just like you lose
your natural color when you leave a tropical
country and come to a city where the sun
feels like it's constipated Ask Lucy Comancho
She knows about all this
art this
artis.

GEOGRAPHY OF THE TRINITY CORONA

Granada Gypsy tongue sucks salt water
Red fish gitana de Granada
Sings
Romany de Hindus
Romany de Hindus
Ibericos boats from the soul
Boats from Ibericos lust
Schizophrenic ships search golden dust
Ladinos
Ladinos
Ancient Spanish
Ancient Spanish
Lengua del Kabala
Kabala lengua
O Mohamet* flor del este
Flor este del Mohamet*
Sonrisa of same people
Flor de Maya
Lengua primordial agua y sal
Mora eyes of paradise
Gypsy freeway
Gypsy freeway
Mohamet*
Ladinos
Romany de Hindus
Valencia
Where sound parked in the tongue
Galicia con pan
Pan Galicia
Pan pan Ibericos
Bridge made of white handkerchiefs
To the cascabels of Andalusia
Walking light the on the loose
Gone through the strings of sitars
Guitars / Sitars
My strings are here

* Peace be upon him

A si
Cadiz   camara my friends
In the pupils of time
jump barefoot into the circle dance
Here comes the Romanies
Islamicals
The Rock of Gibraltar
Rock of Tarik
Like the wave of the ocean
After retreat
On the sand it leaves pearls
From the bottom
Shaped like three-dimensional mandalas

Take my boat
Take my boat

Malaga gitanos
jump the Arawaks
The michicas
Who had gold like we have the air
Golden halos
Of Maya Cocos
Tainos skidding through
Carib sea on canoes
Church pierced the mountain
Gallelocos everywhere
Cement came down from heaven
Taino areyto echoes from the flora
Gone through the pipe of time
Into the face
Into the cheek so cute
España danza
Africoco bembe
Burundanga mixture is the word
Bembe Mohamet* Areyto
Layered peacock cake
Sandwich of language
Take my boat
Take my boat

* Peace be upon him

Yoruba y Arare
Lucumi
Cascabels of Romany gypsies
Nativo antillano
Hindus
Gallegos
Africano
Caribe
Rhythmic circle
The islands are beads
of a necklace
Tarot cards with tobacco smoke
Crescent moon
The handshake of Fatima
Golden and red hot rubies
Chains where sacraments hang
Symphony of
Gypsy flamenco
Fans opening like sound
Out of the acoustic mama bass
Streets of Islam wrapped in
Catholic robes
Where they say an eye for an eye
Teeth for teeth
Jump for jump
Make my Spanish lamp
Make my Spanish lamp
Walk the camels into the gardens
Electric flowers
See them shine
Make my Indian time
Make my Indian time
Song is memory
Memory is song
Take my boat
Take my boat
Make my African alphabet
Skin on skin
Make my African alphabet
Skin on skin
Morocos Africaos

Look the street is full of
Ethiopians
Look Jersey City full of
Tainos
Gitanos lindos
Lucumi inside Yucaye
White angels come from
Arare drums
Visual spectacle envied
by rainbow
Look Pakistani mambo
The cars are the musical race
Even polish my Polish
Mazurka in the guava villages
Blood vessels of combined chemistry
From everywhere to someone
Galicia
Romany de Hindus
Arawaki
Arare

Moro
Lucumi
Ibericos
Mohammedans*
Gypsy
Arabiscus
Yoruba
Tainos
Colors turn into sounds
We start building cities
From blueprints
Found in the sails
Of remember

Take my boat
Take my boat

* Peace be upon him

Ironing Goatskin

The air is suffocating
In the altar which is the sky
The sun the only statue
On this beach the vibrations
Of the drums
The fat barrels of the Bomba
The Papa, the Mama, and the Niño
The way the sound goes up
Your head goes seaward on canucas
Listen
Mercy for the goat flesh, please
The drummers look at the
Mahogany legs of the girls
Who enter the round Bomba circle
And proceed to imitate them
Turning the visual into sound
There isn't a place to sit your
Lungs down
It is for this reason
That we should be concerned
With the destiny of goats.

Two Guitars

Two guitars were left in a room all alone
They sat on different corners of the parlor
In this solitude they started talking to each other
My strings are tight and full of tears
The man who plays me has no heart
I have seen it leave out of his mouth
I have seen it melt out of his eyes
It dives into the pores of the earth
When they squeeze me tight I bring
Down the angels who live off the chorus
The trios singing loosen organs
With melodious screwdrivers
Sentiment comes off the hinges
Because a song is a mountain put into
Words and landscape is the feeling that
Enters something so big in the harmony
We are always in danger of blowing up
With passion
The other guitar:
In 1944 New York
When the Trio Los Panchos started
With Mexican & Puerto Rican birds
I am the one that one of them held
Tight   like a woman
Their throats gardenia gardens
An airport for dreams
I've been in theaters and cabarets
I played in an apartment on 102nd street
After a baptism pregnant with women
The men flirted and were offered
Chicken soup
Echoes came out of hallways as if from caves
Someone is opening the door now
The two guitars hushed and there was a
Resonance in the air like what is left by
The last chord of a bolero.

Mountain Building

The mountains have changed to buildings
Is this hallway the inside of a stem
That has a rattling flower for a head,
Immense tree bark with roots made out of
Mailboxes?
In the vertical village moons fly out of
Apartment windows and though what you
See is a modern city
The mountain's guitars pluck inside
It's agriculture taking an elevator
Through urban caves which lead to
Paths underground They say Camuy
To Hutuado
Taino subground like the IRT in
Constant motion

The streets take walks in your dark eyes
Seashell necklaces make music in the
Origin of silence
What are we stepping on? Pineapple
Fields frozen with snow
Concrete dirt later the rocks of the
Atlantic
The sculpture of the inner earth
Down there where you thought only worms
And unnamed crocodiles parade
Lefty stands on a corner
Analyzing every seed
Squeezing the walls as he passes
Through at the bottom of the basement
Where the boiler makes heat
The flesh arrives out of a hole
In the mountain that goes up like a
Green wall
Bodies come in making maraca sounds
An invisible map out of the flora
Bees arrive in the vicinity and sing

Chorus while woody woodpeckers make
Women out of trees and place flowers
On their heads
Waterfalls like Hurakan's faucets
Caress the back of Yuquiyu
God to all whose tongues have the
Arawak's echoes

Hallway of graffiti like the master
Cave drawings made by owls when they
Had hands
You see the fish with pyramids inside
Their stomachs
Hanging near the doorways where
San Lazaro turns the keys
Villa Manhattan
Breeze of saint juice made from
Coconuts
Slide down the stairs to your
Belly and like a hypnotized guanabana
You float down the street
And win all your hands at dominoes

The Moros live on the top floor eating
Roots and have a rooster on the roof
Africans import okra from the bodega
The Indians make a base of guava
On the first floor
The building is spinning itself into
a spiral of salsa
Heaven must be calling or the
Residents know the direction
Because there is an upward pull
If you rise too quickly from your seat
You might have to comb a spirit's
Hair
They float over the chimneys
Arrive through the smog
Appear through the plaster of Paris
It is the same people in the windowed
Mountains.

The Physics of Ochun

A group of professional
scientists
from Columbia University
heard that in an old
tenement apartment
occupied by a family
named González
a plaster-of-Paris
statue made in Rome
of Caridad del Cobre
started crying
The scientists
curious as they are
took a ride across
town to investigate
After stating their purpose
and their amazement
they were led to the
room where the statue was
Sure enough it was wet
under the eyes
Overnight, Señora González
told them, it had cried so
much that they were able
to collect a jar full of tears
The scientist almost knocked his
gold-rim glasses off his face
May we have this as a specimen
to study in our laboratory?
She agreed, and they took a taxi
with the jar to Columbia
They went directly to the lab
to put the tears through a
series of tests
They put a good amount of
the liquid under their
Strongest Microscope

Lo and behold!
What they saw made them loosen
their neckties
There inside the liquid
clearly made out through
the microscope was the
word: JEHOVAH
No matter how much they
moved the water they
kept getting the word
They sent for a bottle of
scotch
They served themselves in test tubes
They called the González family
to see if they could explain
All the González family knew
was that it was the tears
of Caridad del Cobre
They explained to Señora González
what was happening
She said that weirder than that
was the fact that her
window had grown a staircase
that went up beyond the clouds
She said she and her daughter
had gone up there to check it
out
because, she told them, a
long white rope had come out
of their belly buttons and some-
thing was pulling them up
What happened? the enthusiastic
scientists from Columbia University
wanted to know
We went up there and were
massaged by the wind
We got hair permanents
and our nails manicured
into a purple red
My daughter says she saw

a woodpecker designing the
air
The scientists put the phone down
and their eyes orbited the room
We have to get out there
Incredible things are happening
They rushed back out
and into the González residency
They entered
It's in the same
room with the statue
They rushed in and went to the
window
So amazed were they
they lost their speech
All their organs migrated an inch
Clearly in front of them
a 3-foot-wide marble stair
that went up into the sky
The scientists gathered themselves
to the point of verbalizing again
They each wanted to make sure
that the other was "cognizant"
of the espectacolo
Once they settled upon reality
they decided that the urge to
explore was stronger than their
fears
One decided to take a writing pad
to take notes
One decided to take a test tube
in case he ran into substances
One decided to take a thermometer
and an air bag to collect atmosphere
Señora González, would you please
come up with us?
They wanted to know if she would
lead them up
If you could see it you could touch
it, she told them

She went out first and they
followed
The marble steps were cold
They could have been teeth of
the moon
As they went up the breeze smiled
against their ears
The murmur of the streets dimmed
They were climbing and climbing
when they felt a whirlpool in
the air
For sure it was the hairdresser
Señora González sensed the odor of
many flowers in the breeze
The scientist with the test tube
saw it get full of a white liquid
The scientist with the air bag
felt it change into a chunk of metal
The scientist with the writing pad
saw a language appear on it backwards
printing faster than a computer
The paper got hot like a piece of
burning wood
and he dropped it down into the
buildings
It went through an open window
and fell into a pot of red beans
A woman by the name Concepción was
cooking
Frightened she took it to a doctor's
appointment she had the next day
She showed it to the physician
who examined it
He thought it was the imprint
of flower petals
so even and bold in lilac
ink
The dream Concepción had during
the night came back to her
I know what's going on, doctor

I'll see you in nine months
Walking she remembered forgetting
to put the calabaza into the beans
and rushed home sparkling in
her yellow dress

HERE
      IS AN EAR
HEAR

> *Is the ocean really inside seashells*
> *or is it all in your mind?*
>   —PICHON DE LA ONCE

Behold and soak like a sponge.
I have discovered that the island of Puerto Rico
is the ears of Saru-Saru, a poet reputed to have lived
in Atlantis. On the day that the water kissed and
embraced and filled all the holes of that giant
missing link, this bard's curiosity was the greatest
for he kept swimming and listening for causes.
He picked up rocks before they sank and blew
wind viciously into them. Finally he blew so hard
into a rock that he busted his ear drums; angry,
he recited poems as he tried turning into a bird
to fly to green Brazil. His left ear opened up
like a canal and a rock lodged in it. Rock attracts
rock and many rocks attached to this rock. It got
like a rocket. His ear stayed with it in a horizontal
position. Finally after so many generations he got
to hear what he most wanted: the sounds made by flowers
as they stretched into the light. Behold, I have
discovered that the island of Puerto Rico is the
ears of Saru-Saru.

Groenburgewal Straat

para Steef Davidson y Gea Stadig,
Dutch divinadores

Three ducks in caravan sail by
On the canal which swallows street
The street swallows water and feet
Old buildings leaning from the
Weight of the sky

Cold makes your mind be a boat
in the Carib sea
Ducks with buds in water
Stride with brushes on their beaks
Free from shivers and this
Radiator heat

Paint themselves hanging, at
The Rysk Museum next to bread
and wine
Lunch is on the walls
Guards patrol make sure
You don't bring spoon or knife

It seems that a Dutch Master
Insulted a passing man
The man went home and got a
Blade
He cut one and punched another
Out
The others ran for muskets

Amsterdam is round like a
Pancake
Streets make hooks loops
And circles into each other
They seem to rotate
Whole sections relocate

On the streets Indonesian
Jade
Percolating out of Edam cheese
Curaçao coconut bridge
Colonialism is always
Take and get
Energy colonizes the cream

The sounds of gongs
Announce the coming
Down a canal of
The craftsmen of the
Ancient Pacific boats
The inventors of paper
Rice fingers
Bells which unite
With streams in the blood
Awake the people

The moon is a round
Gouda
Its dress is the water
That circulates
The ancient village

Where everyone is always
Recreating on bicycles
Light blasting out
of red hair

This constant merry-go-round
Ah, where is this
Amsterdamn

Borinkins in Hawaii

For Norma Carr, Blaise Sosa,
and Ayala and his famous corner

In 1900
A ship left San Juan Harbor
Full of migrant workers
Of the fields
Enroute to what they believed
To be California
Instead something like C & H
Which managed the vessel
With strings like a puppet
From afar
Took them to Hawaii

When Toño who was one of them
And Jaime who was another
And Felipe who was a third
Of the many 8,000 who took
This spin
Saw Hawaii they thought they
Were still in Puerto Rico
It took movement of time
Show up of the wind
It took the Japanese currents
To convince them
That in somewhere they were

Sugar was the daddy on the
Commercial horizon
Donuts for everybody
Ah history was getting sweet
If you wasn't a cane worker
With sores on your feet
And corns on your hands
Under the sun for how much
A day
Sugar was gonna blow flesh up

Sugar mania
Sugar comes from cane
Get some cane
Get some workers
Get some land

The United States talked to the
Old Hawaiian queen
It was a polite conversation
The gringo merely pointed
To where the Marines
Were casually placed
Just that
The Hawaiian Kingdom
Pieces of cake
Littered on the Pacific

"What in the mountain got
Into you Toño to wanna come
From where you were
To jump on this boat
To come to this other planet.
Look a volcano to lite your
Cigar, a desert for your
Camel, what is this the
End of the world, HA."

"Well Jaime look a guava
And coconut is coconut
See that tree where a Pana
Hangs. Smell the flowers
Fragrance like Aibonito"
Thru each Pana-pen a metropopis
Of juices and texture
Ulus are Pana-pens in Puerto Rico
Ulus: Hawaii
Pana-pen: Puerto Rico
Breadfruit for you
Ulus hang like earrings
From the ears of women

On the trees
A blue dress on top
The curve is the horizon
A reminder that we all live
On a Pana-pen

Hawaii feudal 19th century
Catholic liturgy
Thru the flower tops
The best years of
Tomas-Toñon
Jaime
Felipe and the full migration
Living in camps
Box homes for workers
And their families
Early risers
Church on Sunday
Machete on Monday
Orange curtains thru
The greenery
Cuatro strings
With the bird speech
The pick pickers of
Pineapple stress the
Decima
As back in Borinkin
Ya se men
In ten lines you hem
A skirt
In Kohala they call it
Cachy-cachy
People jumpy-jumpy
Like roosters
The cuatro guitar chirps
Squeeky its note in the
Upper C high nose pitch
Sound of the Arawak
Garganta of the Areyto
Song gallery of the

Ancient inhabitants
Of the boat Borinkin

Broken guitars navigating
Vessels
Arrive like seed onto the
Ground
Whatever is in the dirt
Will come out
We're gonna finger pop
The pineapple
The cane is gonna fly
The mayordomos will whip
Ankles
Secret hidden wood
Will get them
There are dark passages of night
Roads under the kona trees
In the dark the sound kaploosh
On the skull
The mayordomos are paid
By the plantation owners
The wood is made by nature

At Ayalas Place
3rd & 4th generation Puerto Rican
Hawaiians
Eat rice and beans prepared
By Japanese woman
Soya sauce on the tables
Hawaii only Puerto Rican
Oriental community in the
World

A ship which left San Juan
Turn of the century
Transported workers music
And song
They thought they were
California bound

But were hijacked by
Corporate agriculture
Once they got to land
They folded over
They grew and mixed
Like Hawaii can mix
Portuguese sausage slit
Inside banana leaf
Filipino Japanese eyes
Stare from mulatto faces

The Portuguese brought
The ukulele to anxious fingers
Who looked at the motion of
Palm leaves to help them search
For a sound
They studied the designs of
The hula dancers
And made
A guitar which sounds like
It's being played by the
Fingers of the breeze
They all dance cachy-cachy
And jumpy-jumpy
In places like Hilo
And Kohala
You hear the shouts
You hear the groans
You feel the wind of the
Cane workers' machete
And in the eyes you see
The waves of the oceans
You see beads
Which form a necklace
Of islands
Which have emerged out of
The tears.

from

red beans

1991

RED MEANS

Red be-ings
whose history is
Adam's apple
Guyaba at the
entrance
To the cave
Which Lucifer
Entered to
Terminate with
darkness
Taking that ride
up the throat
Finding the stove
of the kitchen
Where someone
Had been up earlier
Cooking Red Beans

Snaps of Immigration

1

I remember the fragrance of
the Caribbean
A scent that anchors into the
ports of technology.

2

I dream with suitcases
full of illegal fruits
Interned between white
guayaberas that dissolved
Into snowflaked polyester.

3

When we saw the tenements
our eyes turned backwards
to the miracle of scenery
At the supermarket
My mother caressed the
Parsley.

4

We came in the middle of winter
from another time
We took a trip into the future
A fragment of another planet
To a place where time flew
As if clocks had coconut oil
put on them.

5

Rural mountain dirt walk
Had to be adjusted to cement
pavement
The new city finished the
concrete supply of the world
Even the sky was cement
The streets were made of shit.

6
The past was dissolving like
sugar at the bottom of a coffee cup
That small piece of earth that
we habitated
Was somewhere in a television
Waving in space.

7
From beneath the ice
From beneath the cement
From beneath the tar
From beneath the pipes and wires
Came the cucurucu of the roosters.

8
People wrote letters as if they
were writing the scriptures
Penmanship of women who made
tapestry with their hands
Cooked criollo pots
Fashioned words of hope and longing
Men made ink out of love
And saw their sweethearts
Wearing yellow dresses
Reaching from the balcony
To the hands of the mailman.

9
At first English was nothing
but sound
Like trumpets doing yakity yak
As we found meanings for the words
We noticed that many times the
Letters deceived the sound
What could we do
it was the language of a
foreign land.

New/Aguas Buenas/Jersey

In the forties the populace was sucking on barb
wire
Cans found on the streets were squeezed to the
maximum
Hot air moving through wooden houses
They were Bohíos
We were Tainos
It's Areyto moving down from Sumidero
Pouring in from Caguitas
Inside the living rooms Aguasboneses walked
on compressed dirt
They made it shine
Cooked on kerosene stoves
Says the elders they woke up with stained noses
The chemical odor did them in
For that reason they lived in the streets
They lived in the mountains
Go home to eat and sleep
Roosters mounted chickens at random under
houses
For the children the toys were the insects
and sing songs from the time of Spain
Closer than Spain was the pain
People survived with the beauty of the song
The hidden gracious heart
That love that loved whoever it was
We carry our blood
Even toward destructions
And what else could it be
An army to fight destiny: for what in the matter
The families collapsed like red flowers
off of flamboyan trees.

The Spanish wanted gold first.
The priest wanted converts.
Sailors have always wanted pussy.

The Taino kingdoms melted in the mountains
The Areytos into the bone marrow to mix with
The juices of semen to that now generation
Our faces aboriginal designs

The island was purgatory
The retina saw in flora and fauna the spirit half
The same way a chest or a cross is visible
It was our materialism
The Spaniards came with so much embroidery
Our virgins were naked
This is a climate for flesh
Up in Mula thrown on a hammock receiving wind
upon my testicles
Aroma of azucena jumps only at night
The same as La Siciliana who only opens
within the darkness
In the eyes of the plaza I can still
see the nakedness pouring out
The heat invites us to take off our clothes
Imagine such polyester melted by the
primal sun

I am moving in the tensions with the tenses
History hanging within long skirts
The Black Virgin La Montserrate on a passage
Through the center of a town of wooden
Houses painted blue, green, yellow, pink,
orange
Black shawls and white hats
Join the rivers, the trees, the frogs,
and the rain which is about to fall
And the rain which is about to fall
Rain
In adoration of an image

The island was abandoned by history
Only the sun fell upon a coast of Andaluz
Spaniards who improvised a government
Accusing others of the crimes they committed

To settle Taino yucayeyes they went deeper
inland
With flashes of Moorish and Visigothic
harmonics
Made paths through the guayaba flavor

Avicenna and ibn 'Arabi in costume at the
festival Bomba y Plena
Pineapple in Baghdad Morococo

The silence of the past
Rules the manifestations of the future
The spirits are in charge here
Who comes through Guánica
Who comes through San Juan Bay
Who comes through airport
Doesn't know how ridiculous
the riddle can get

The space was exported
as industry was imported
The campesinos were taken into the future
There was only past and future
There was no now
The Marine Tiger left
Sumidero Mula Caguitas
La Pajilla El Guanabano
went to Newark Avenue
Bergen Montgomery
Grove
Sixth Street
There was nothing to do in Aguas Buenas
But to stare into the mountain Jagueyes
There was no government
No plans for agriculture
The plans were for tourist
and pharmaceutical companies
The people who dropped the bomb on
Hiroshima came from the North
The methods were different

but the clearing was the same
A beautiful house with no one in it

Jersey City take the path back
To the island of vegetation
Let us retrogress into the future.

SCARLET SKIRT

I terminated with the color red
when this vibrant hue pressed against
me up on a mountaintop
Upon which I didn't know how I got
Drunk and in pursuit of a scarlet
skirt that had made a passage through
a festive plaza
It started the way it started
but don't ask me how that was
Rum and 98 degrees is a devastation
of the senses
Through her lips she gleamed a yes
And with that yes we went off on
a journey onto a street to the point
where cement ran out
And the red dirt began
The night was choking the daylight
out of the atmosphere
You could still count the coquís
which had started their nightly
Glee club
We didn't hold hands
But in the sway of the walk our pinkies
would brush against each other
In midair
She told me her name but it was
already the point when the bottle
Of rum was beyond the halfway mark
So all I could do now is speculate
Was it Nilsa, or Elena or Julia
Just plain and thrown
Or was it Anna-María, Sonia Carmin
Something with more combustive
Syllables
Or was it a much more rural name
Like Blasina or Amparo
It is all now in the flow of the

river that we might have passed
En route toward a singular light
At the very top of the earth
Which was her house
This part of the path was full
Of rocks which turned out to be
frogs
For they would take leaps
In front of my foolish head
Which by now had more rum
Than the bottle
The sounds of animals
The soft breeze
The crescent moon
Convinced us to sit on a
fallen tree
Her legs dispersed out of
her scarlet skirt in various
Curves
As we spoke little episodes
of our histories
I shot flurries of warm moisture
into her ears
And then as quick as a lizard's
head she stood up
Saying I must go
disappeared into the darkness
The tail of a cow which had
been watching us from a distance
Did more than us
There I was in the sullen shade
of night holding an empty
Bottle of rum far from the
center of town in an elevation
Which I knew not
Composing myself I threw the bottle
away and took direction
My head in the misty heaven of
sugar cane
Singing the opening lines of one

bolero after another
Lo I came upon a fork in the road
Going is never like coming
A pause of indecision
The whole Caribbean stood still
I just went in the direction I heard
less frogs and coquís
Thinking myself en route toward
civilization
After some paces I found the hole
of my life
I fell down a precipice like
a clown in a movie
With my white apparel I cleaned
the side of the mountain
And fell into a gathering of
guava bushels
There I was drunk and dizzy
crimson from the mud I had
Rolled on
I shitted twice on the cipher 10
and continued my journey into
Town
At long last I found the lights
of the beginning
Soon I was crossing the plaza
It must've been one in the morning
I looked like a potato that had
been internalized in a pot of
Red beans
I made a turn on the street
leading to my home
Suddenly I saw a figure of
good dimensions standing next
To the gate
It was not human but a beast
I came a little closer and
registered that it was in fact
A bull
Tremendous bullshit

I found a rock and threw it in its
direction to see if it would scatter
Away
But it was immobile
It just stood there waiting as
if I owed it some money
I had to find an alternate way
of getting to my bed
I went through a side street
and climbed the stairs of
Don Berencho's house which gave me access
to the roof of the house next to
mine
This put me in jumping distance
onto the back balcony of my house
I swore that I had left the door
open
Once I jumped and turned the knob
it told me something else
it had been closed
I thought of yelling to my sister
But I reviewed my condition
Drunk
Bumps and scratches all over
And my clothes looked as if I'd
just climbed out of a pot of
Red beans
What words could be occupied as
an explanation?

I laid myself out on an old
rattan sofa that we had there
The thought of the scarlet skirt
beat me to sleep
It is such an expensive color
it's the heat of our passions
I terminated with the color red
After descending from the
mountaintop.

PROBLEMS WITH HURRICANES

A campesino looked at the air
And told me:
With hurricanes it's not the wind
or the noise or the water.
I'll tell you he said:
it's the mangoes, avocados
Green plantains and bananas
flying into town like projectiles.

How would your family
feel if they had to tell
The generations that you
got killed by a flying
Banana.

Death by drowning has honor
If the wind picked you up
and slammed you
Against a mountain boulder
This would not carry shame
But
to suffer a mango smashing
Your skull
or a plantain hitting your
Temple at 70 miles per hour
is the ultimate disgrace.

The campesino takes off his hat—
As a sign of respect
toward the fury of the wind
And says:
Don't worry about the noise
Don't worry about the water
Don't worry about the wind—
If you are going out
beware of mangoes
And all such beautiful
sweet things.

An Essay on William Carlos Williams

I love the quality of the
spoken thought
As it happens immediately
uttered into the air
Not held inside and rolled
around for some properly
schemed moment
Not sent to circulate a cane
field
Or on a stroll that would include
the desert and Mecca
Spoken while it happens
Direct and pure
As the art of salutation
of mountain campesinos come to
the plaza
The grasp of the handshake upon
encounter and departure
A gesture unveiling the occult
behind the wooden boards of
your old house
Remarks show no hesitation
to be expressed
The tongue itself carries
the mind
Pure and sure
Sudden and direct
like the appearance
of a green mountain
Overlooking a town.

Areyto

My empire of flamboyans
Through boulevards made of mountains
Dressed green to the heavens
As voices circulate the hymns
of our history
From the dancers of the round
serpent formed at the center of
Life
This is Americas Areyto
This is Americas Areyto

In cities mountains of flying metallic
cars and consumer junk/
Nerves pile up upon horizons
of progress
That whisper inside/
Mira look
Look mira that whisper inside
Is the old calendar ticking
The Areyto is still swinging:
The Gods said they would take
us back and deliver us from
Plush media inventions
From racket and industrial tension
From textbooks that are lying
tongues of pretensions
The river on the other side
of English is carrying the message
Yukiyu has not abandoned you
The quetzals are still flying
Quetzalcóatl is on the phone
Be cool Roberto and José
Carmen and María
Just go horizontal into the circle
Areyto

The current will take you

America that Betances, José Martí
That Hostos wanted all together as
ONE
Vasconcelos said RAZA CÓSMICA
Seeing red mixed with black
And black with white
Rhythms united married in history
This is the greatest flavor
The earth has to offer

Marimba tango samba
Danza Mambo bolero

Linda America just rise and take
off your clothes
Your age is so old that
Giants appear out of trees as tobacco
smoke takes photographs of the wind
Directing itself into a voice
Where salt pebbles dance guaguancó
Something so good that it became
blueprint for legs
That moved with such precision
That ten thousand appear to be one
In the Areyto where you hear the drum
As the knees and the legs
describe an area between two stars

Old fire of agricultural guitar
spreading North
Trio Los Diamantes sunrise moving
through silk on slow tropical wind
Johny Albino Trio San Juan
Making an escalator of sound
Into your hearts that grow feathers
To fly toward the desert to enter
The la'uds invasion of Iberian perfume
To land upon the shoulders of Gypsies

and Mayas as a fan from Granada cools
our Amerindian features of the love
That comes of the love that goes

America is our belly
Our abdomen of spirit
We grew out of the plants
It knows who we are
Linda America that Betances
José Martí to Hostos us up UNIDOS
As único one (JUAN)

America sur south
America norte
Juan America
Two America Juan
Juan America one
Then America blend
Give the idea roots of
harmonious peace serene/
Sí and yes it is possible for the
Snake of heart and mind to
grow quetzal feathers and fly
Out of the Areyto circle
Areyto circle
Areyto dance

Possible to be possible
Possible to be
A whole unto one
A nation with lots of fish to
eat
And fruit that offers itself
it is possible to be
it is possible to
Struggle against blocks
of inertia
Against conquistadors' wishes
lurking in blood nervous systems
Nightmaring dreams/

Dogs that come bark at the
beautiful dance
It is possible to be
pure fresh river water
We are bird that sings
Free

Areyto
Maraca güiro and drum
Quicharo maraca y tambor
Who we are
Printed in rhythm and song

Areyto south
Areyto North
Two America Juan
One America One
America that Bolívar Betances
to José Martí Us to Hostos who wanted
us to be one único Unidos

Areyto güiro and drum
Quicharo maraca y tambor

Areyto song
Areyto song
AREYTO.

1993

El Poema de lo Reverso

In which everything goes backward
in time and motion
Palm trees shrink back into the ground
Mangos become seeds
and reappear in the eyes of Indian
women
The years go back
cement becomes wood
Panama hats are seen upon skeletons
walking the plazas
Of once again wooden benches
The past starts to happen again
I see Columbus's three boats
going backwards on the sea
Getting smaller
Crossing the Atlantic back to the
ports of Spain   Cadiz   Dos Palos   Huelva
Where the sailors disembark
and go back to their towns
To their homes
They become adolescents again
become children   infants
they re-enter the wombs of their mothers
till they become glances
Clutching a pound of bread
through a busy plaza
that becomes the taste
of the sound of church bells
in reverberation.

ILIACION

y but I know
the soft entrance
you always give
sweat and abandoned
there is no problem
with you
this is all there
as we in it put
you await only the moment
hunger like eye have
felt in my own entrails—
chew quick and swallow
A desperation
Of our own needs
Surmount—
Slave of mine
dedicate yourself
To all vanishment
Hurt and all want
This water for salt
that only makes more thirst
give the very nothing of it all
a god inside of a fruit
Released from a window
How could possible thought
eat itself
From the aerial vocabulary
Which from the sound you
could sprinkle
hysterical murmurs
In the insignificance
we communicate
what is this want
That came as if
Liberating something
that was blocked/A pipe

A drainage
Then flowing in the hurt
embarrassed and foul mouth
Sucia
Mente montage
Mound of Iliacion
Iluminada
Agua en el coco
the revelation occupied
All the sacred exterior
the very ether must fight
to surround you
y i y lala
Swallow whole portions
of each other
till we are not seen
only sound is present
y a and me la—aí.

Segunda ola

primero el viento pasa por tí
sin tu darte cuenta
conocimiento—eres tu corriendo
por lo pasado invisible
es así que te das cuenta
que te miro
te miro como miro al mirar
sabrás que te mido
al pasar el paso
qué paso
ves que varias estrellas se apagaron
notas donde se fue la luz
tocas algo que no es materia
tocas algo que no es espíritu
que es tu ombligo
visión en mi lengua
el sabor que te dejo
lo explica

que estás despierta en un sueño
o que estás viva y lista

despierta/dormida
dormida/despierta

¿Cuál?

Ajonjolí

If you want movement,
If you want passage,
If you want current,
That is if you need whirlpool,
Velocity,
A glow flow ultrasonic,
Thrust,
Dash,
A gush of frenesi . . .
Well then Ajonjolí.

DIMENSIONS OF A LINGUIST

I felt it in Taino
I thought about it in Spanish
I wrote it in English.

Red Beans

Next to white rice
it looks like coral
sitting next to snow

Hills of starch
border
The burnt sienna
of irony

Azusenas being chased by
the terra cotta feathers
of a rooster

There is a lava flow
through the smoking
white mounds

India red
spills on ivory

Ochre cannon balls
falling
next to blanc pebbles

Red beans and milk
make burgundy wine

Violet pouring
from the eggshell
tinge of the plate.

SUITE

I know what I did was wrong
But the wrong was on the earth
And I found myself amongst it
I have deciphered now its rhythms
And away from it I dance
I have told the spirits
To do with me what they will
I have explained to them
And they have responded
Take care of your concerns
Or a river of piranhas
Will flow through your eyes
I know you are me
And have also betrayed yourselves
Let us work together
Like seeds inside a maraca
I know I have done wrong
Slowly I walk back home
What are you doing?

* * *

I'm going to dress up
First I'm going to wash myself in the river
I'm going to get myself some red shoes
And I'm going to make me a hat
Out of all the words I have written
And uttered in the past
I'm going to call a woman that wants to dance
I'm going to whistle for some birds to come
And sit on my shoulders
I'm going to pluck their feathers and place
Them on my hat
Into the jungle I'll go for some bamboo
And make a cane to walk into the plaza with

Let me know if you hear what I say
Sharpen the spurs of the roosters
From the palms I'll get some coconut oil
And shine my hair for the night
For tonight is the birthdate
Of the saint that watched my birth
The Black Virgin
Virgin Morena, Reina de Cataluña
La Monserrate
From the horses I will pick
A fine-stepping Arabian
I am going to dress up
The invisible body of my song.

* * *

A lizard signals to a butterfly,
ears that dance by flowers,
the colors crumble into sound,
a hunger beyond mouth.
I am before Columbus in a hut,
Where the memory is larger than
the cathedrals of Toledo,
Into the dusk trees
beams the moon of centuries
for evidence I bring you a tortoise,
discuss with it the way
you measure a season,
Reptile
Caterpillar
observe a flying flower
The words from the macaw's beak
In the memory hammock
Swaying.

* * *

In the meters of the octavals
Zejels of the crescent moon,
Cordoba or Aibonito
in its festival of flowers,
the scental rose of her eyes,
that point better than a finger.
Deeper into the gourd
a circle of red syllables,
juices of oranges and pineapples
substituting the ink of the plume
The Inca pluma
Below a cloud of Lime
following the composer
of "La Flor de la Canela"
through the Alameda,
The intuition of the mass
in the air.
And have you seen this bird
in flight
a book of feathers.

from

letters from the island

1995-2000

poems written with children in mind
dedicated to my daughter Kairi

[THIS IS MY LELOLAI]

This is my lelolai
it is the year 1850
women walk with long
skirts,
Men's hats are straw
and pra-pras
with ribbons around them
Distances would be greater
for it was foot and horse.
The North Americans had
not arrived,
No dollars it was pesos.
The agriculture was coffee
sugar cane   tobacco.
A man from France
Oui Oui brought the café
bean to Martinique
And it kept growing
moving to all the other
islands of floating mountains
Being pierced by the sun,
in red Caribbean soil
made an espresso of tongues
Flavor with morning bread.
Island coffee went all
over Europe,
Parisians strolling with canes
in Yauco markets
Hacienda vistas mango and bamboo
"merci beaucoup"
Melting in the sun.
No machines but hands,
seed, harvest
once again hands in the
earth
Sinking into red dirt
as mosquitos made feast

on skin,
It was an island sun of
long slow days
What existed in the world came
upon boats.
Children had to walk to
school if there was one
miles away
From a high panorama
from which they could
see the curves of eternity.

[RAIN]

Rain
Blue sky
Heat rises
Moving white clouds
To a corner
Wind blows them
Back gray,
Afternoon
Rain
The sound of thick
Drops
A distant mountain
Still blue sky
The eve
Comes in with stars,
Pineapple light,
Tamarindo taste breeze
A green that's
Dark purple.
Once again Rain
Like a lullaby
To sleep.
Rain.

[THERE WAS A PIRATE]

There was a pirate
famous all along the
coast of contraband
The Spanish ships were always
after him,
his name was Cofresi,
They would see him in San Juan
same time they would see
him in Cabo Rojo,
A ship would appear on
the horizon,
Looking again it was but
a whale rising out of
the water,
The people of the west
coast of the island
say that he was like Robin Hood
stealing from the rich
and giving to the poor.
All the countries of Europe,
England, Holland, France,
Portugal were all around,
everybody wanted to get a beautiful
tropical island,
Ah, green emeralds floating,
up for grabs for who has
the most guns,
No one on them but vanishing natives,
it was the late 1700s
there was no television
People got the stories late,
way after they happened,
Women with no shoes washing
clothes in the rivers
Banging them against the rocks,
they say the people hid Cofresi.
 He was captured in Ponce

gathering men to go off to
sea again,
He was wearing clothes
he had taken off the Dutch
and the French,
His fingers were full of Spanish
rings,
He was taken to San Juan,
behind the medieval walls
Where the Castilians
ate no stories.

KAIRI: PAINTING

Gaviotas flying like
white handkerchiefs
below the sky blue
their long necks
the shape of a question
mark
As if asking all the human
sight see:
How come you are stuck
to the ground
The soil of your thoughts
hurry out of the fuss
and write to the rhythm
of my wings a poem
of remembrance
Become the slow traveler
of love.

Thinking of you from the
distance
I am in the footstep
you just took
Not the foot nor the step
do I miss
The shadow before the leather
encloses it
The instinct of disappearance,
see again how we used to skip
together down the street
So many onces now forever.

There you are in all the
corners of a house giggling
Laughing with your chocolate
flavor
Asking the question of nature
The way you ask me what is what

of why is where
It's an adventure you can paint
like the gaviotas flying
toward the mountains green
It's adventure
mystery and fun
Make of it new birds
make new colors for the feathers
within a frame of liberation.

from White Table

How a lizard hears
the flies and bees as a concert
of dance and music
Before they look
making the actual sight
Just a verification
of their imaginations.
The odor of papaya
guanabana and green
Plantains such olfato
eaten through flesh
The little reptile
has then a bird's eye
View of where it is frozen
The female is so such,
before seeing the distance
The air is weighed
and explained to the horse.

Midnight
the air and the rocks
are divided
The instinct
between the air and the wind
It was when I left
the story to tell a fish
The contents
It was then that I hit
a sharp stone.
The fish went on its
way up river
And continued the story for me
as a body washed down river
To feed the sharks
of the ocean.

Those are the dangers
of losing the story line.

An iceberg fell into the room
from the sky
Clear through ice with no veins
so cold it was
That all fell back with shivers
How did such such get here
It needs all the stars
to become candles

The thing was lain out
Within a square of burning
fires

It was wired up with plants
and olive oil—it was smoked
With frankincense and slammed
with Bibles

Not a gulp of humidity
Not a thought of water
They hooked it into copper
Horses started to jump over it

Then it coughed
Someone threw a white cloth
The inferno jumped out of the ice
it turned into a cabaret
Breaking ice for rum
It started to hop and gallop
all around the room
It took everything with it
The flight was booked
into the Orient.

It is enough to receive
the words
which are poison
Without the accompaniment

of the lips.
This is why
there is a system
of armed guards
at the intersections
Guiding newly
arrived tourists
Before vampires
get to the lingering
smell of recently
abandoned blood.

But a pebble here sits and waits
But a small stone sits and waits
A tree sits and waits
A shell thrown from the abdomen
of the sea sits and waits
A gourd waits patiently
to be turned into a maraca
A pearl reposes in mucus
and waits to be discovered
Everything sits and waits
A precious locale never seen
Waits
I've upon one come
throw me your eyes
I will take you to a ledge of Jaqueyes
a mountain that waits by a house
Where upon the table
the ink waits
the candle
the water
the cigar
the rhythm
Sits and waits
for the arrival of the poetry.

Root of Three

I walk in New York with a mountain
in my pocket
I walked in Puerto Rico with a guitar
in my belly
I walked in Spain with Mecca
in my sandals
I invented the theory of guayaba
Humacao turned it into a seed
gave it to a woman
Who dove into a hole in the ground
with it
She came back in seven days
with a round yellow fruit
In Ifa land I was a cane
for the poets of divination
I saw blood cells
moonlight as drumbeats

I floated Uranus
when the earth was a sheet of paper
In the book of sparkles
each ray of light
Became a letter
each letter a mineral
The language of the sea is turquoise
I noticed this walking to Dorado
From where I took a horse
into the waves

I walk in New York with a fan
in my pocket
Made with the feathers
of three continents
It blows African feet
It blows Spanish heart
It blows Taino head space

I am the three in one
The father
The son
And the Holy Ghost.

español caribe

1996-1999

AscaracaristikiscaristikiscaristikiscaracalisAscaractiski
tisscatiskitiscatiskitisAscaracatiskitiscatiskitiscarakatis.

Mon Rivera

El trabalengua
de Puerto Rico

Federico García Lorca

A Manuel Fernández-Montesinos
y Laura García Lorca

En España hay calles de piedra
donde el zapateo del cuero ha hecho
tanto sonido.
Un eco que va y viene y se pierde
en la noche de la península
que peina el cabello de África.

Ventanas como guitarras verticales
vibranto el Segovia de tantas miradas.
Brillantes joyas visigodas
piedras rojas en la correa de las espadas
Heraldos armados, roperos de acero
cuando la niña abrió la puerta.

La misma calle ha sido otra lengua
lamiendo otra época
reserva el acento la raíz de
nuestro pelo
madera de barcos ondulando
en las olas de la negrura
sombra de los azulejos poéticos,
fuentes que brotan la sangre
del cielo.

Por el margen de la Alhambra
una estructura-un libro de versos,
en cada salón una esposa joven
preciosa en el aire.
La mezquita con orgullo en su luz
susurra a la creciente luna
ya tejida en el pico de un gallo,
la Sierra Nevada se luce
como un matador amolando
su amor al toro
mientras baja por los canales

agua a bendecir la casa de Alá.

India en los pantalones negros
del flamenco
bailan el sánscrito pito
de las ventanas flautas
de ron Albaicín-
Federico presente bajo las
columnas moras que son sus
piernas saliendo de su boca.

Monolo-Laura
en el molinete de la salsa
en noche de luna traspasada
por el arma blanca del sol,
El caribe bailó con tu sangre
cerca de aquellos versos del Corán,
nuestras almas de donde se
vacía el Orinoco, canoas Guaraní
imágenes de islas desnudas,
Lorca en la rumba de Cuba,
América un error en fonética,
somos gitanos de contrabando,
añoramos la China perdida
y la bella orquídea de la India
(transládence-de Granada a Manatí
ví a Lorca de mano con la sirena
su cintura boricua llena de alfabetos
hablando como plata durante la
puesta del sol).

El teatro de su niñez
la pantalla de Andalucía
y él una página
para los textos de las manos
de su nana.
Oye hay canciones
que nos mesen hasta dormirnos,
Las oimos de nuevo en Harlem
el canto blues hondo de la calle 125

Su desierto azul
que baila hacia los gritos
de las aguas del Río Hudson.
Corona para el rey de Harlem
Corona para el rey de Granada–
Dando a-luz en Fuentevaqueros
Terror y besos
Fuego y rosa.

Agricultor de cosechas de colores
Borges lo bautizó pintor
dibujando con sus palabras
líneas/círculos   llanuras
cavernas ocultas-una nación.

La mirada de un viejo
en los ojos de un niño
el viento de su palabra joven
ya piedra antigua.
Hizo la sinuosa respiración
coger forma,
Como ciudades tan visibles
que hoy caminamos por ellas,
bailamos allá dentro de sus
estrofas
y por ellas vuelan las palomas,
en los cuartos de su poesía
cocinamos nuestra piel.

El nos dejó plazas llenas de deseos,
balcones para el sol de medio día.
El agua y el fuego
La mujer y el hombre,
La falda y los pantalones
y la carretera
Que va hacia el río
para siempre iluminada.

De Tres Raíces

Camino por Nueva York con una montaña
en mi bolsillo
Caminé por Puerto Rico con una guitarra
en mi estómago
Caminé por España con Mecca
en mis sandalias
Inventé la teoría de la guayaba
Humacao la convirtió en una semilla
Se la dió a una mujer
que se la llevó a lo subterráneo
Regresó a los siete días
con una fruta redonda y amarilla
En la tierra de Ifé era un bastón
abrazado por los poetas de profecía
Vi células de sangre
disfrazadas como ritmos de tambor

Floté por Urano
cuando la tierra era una hoja de papel
En el libro de las estrellas
cada rayo de luz
Se tornó una letra
cada letra en un mineral
El lenguaje del mar es color turquesa
me dí cuanta al caminar hacia Dorado
Donde monté caballo
hacia Aguas Buenas

Camino por Nueva York con un abanico
en mi bolsillo
Hecho de plumas
de tres continentes
Sopla pies africanos
Sopla corazón español
Sopla cabeza taína

Soy el tres en uno
El Padre
El Hijo
Y el Espíritu Santo.

BOBADILLA, ESPAÑA

En las caras de Málaga duermen
memorias de Marruecos,
algo del turrón en los ojos,
la boca berebere en el hondo romance.
El mapa de su piel también tiene el
maíz de Vespucci,
ví una joven mestiza como si
saliera del vapor de un nacatamal.
Medir todo con pelo negro,
la distancia del Atlántico,
los barcos como camellos
de madera,
campanas, campanas.
La lengua era una espada
en época remota que se revuelca
en cada mirada.

Una muchachería pasa gritando
Olé, Olé
una coquetería de nueva ropa,
aún las uñas de sus pies sueltan
arena del Sahara.

Sevilla fue el puente del sol,
el otro Tito el caribe mambo,
que brillo toda la noche;
En el club Salamandra al cruzar
la calle del río árabe Quadalquivir
las Sevillanas zapatearon salsa
flamencada, María la Guapa quemándose
la ropa, sancocho con rumba caribéña,
la cintura Macarena, menéala, menéala,
salto del mar la piedra Gilbraltar.

En Córdoba un viejo pide un brandy
con el sol de la mañana,
pasa una rubia de pelo negro,

se inclina sobre el bastón:
" . . . . y la madre que la parió."
Su perfil me recordó de su
contrapunto: un viejo saliendo
de la tabacalera de Caguas,
unos zapatos blancos
pisando unas losetas de patrones
de amapolas abiertas.

En la estación del tren
en Málaga,
la mujer detrás del mostrador
me dijo con tranquilidad:
"El Expresó ya se fue."
Era el tren, el único
para llegar en tiempo
para el vuelo que salía
de Madrid.

Mi cara se convirtió en zumo
de tamarindo,
se dió cuenta ella que hablaba
con un palo de Caoba.
La mujer le metió dedos
a las teclas de la computadora,
me explicó que había un local
que venía como una tortuga
por las vías, podría cogerlo
hasta Bobadilla
y conectar con un local
hacia Madrid, llegaría
por la mañana con tiempo
para llegar al aereopuerto.

Pues me fuí para Bobadilla,
que palabra de pueblo
para sonar tan bonita.

En dos horas de singladura
saltó Bobadilla,

de una bobería de oscuridad
y postes de luces.
Eran las doce de la mañana nada,
el tren para Madrid llegaría
a las 2:30,
me tiré a la plataforma de
la estación
un relente frío de mármol,
como de gato sin comer
en cuento de Juan Rulfo.

Guardé mis maletas y salí
por las calles a mirar ventanas,
por las rajas de una cortina
comtemplé una vieja,
una de esas eternas Doña Jertrudis,
su cara sin la canela del novomunde
antes del mestizaje.
En las paredes cuadros de Vírgenes,
retratos de ancestros.

No pasaba nada en Bobadilla,
silencio y un distante ladrar
de perro o perra.

En la estación el restaurante bar
lleno de tíos locales
que vociferaban imperiales galillos,
caras visigodas armadas como castillos,
sus ojos como torres de cañones.
Otras más celtas en revoltillo
con aires de nariz romana,
cuando no un aplaste gitanillo,
pelo negro y castaño de castañuela
Castilla.

Un marroquí apareció por una puerta,
viajaba solo,
iba hacia Francia
venía chancleteando de Marakesh,

jornada como de antigua costumbre
de caravanas del desierto eterno,
infinitas trazesías por arena y agua.
Luego llegaron dos moras,
una de Argelia la otra de Mauritania,
formamos una instantánea familia.

Los tíos en la distancia cerveseaban
el machismo bolín,
mirando los sentía criticando,
ridiculizando,
el constante goofeo humillante del
Quijote,
corte de espada de la cual no se salvó
el Caribe,
católicos de estatuas de yeso,
Cristo de porcelena,
bañados en aceite de oliva.

Se le ocurre a la muchacha
de Mauritania
preguntarle a uno de los tíos:
"Por qué no cambian el horrible
nombre de este pueblo, qué es
esto de Bobadilla, es una
bobería."

Pero ellos ebrios de cada noche
llenos de jamón y bacalao,
de costumbre y tradición,
defendieron tal ortografía.
Será que viene de Francisco de Bobadilla,
o fue Bobadilla que vino
primero de la bobería de las Indias,
tantas flores que mató en Quisqueya,
colono de tan mala riña,
lo sacaron para otros terrenos,
no sé si regresó de su agreso
a la Penin o si murió enflechado,
o en el fondo de un río

respirando oro en piedra.

Un caribeño y tres moros
bailamos en la plataforma,
oímos la bocina del tren,
una luz como una estrella
que caía hacia nosotros.
En el caballo de hierro
nos reímos, hablando árabe
español y francés.
Pasamos por pueblos
que no estaban en el mapa,
quítate de la vía Perico
que hacia el norte sube
el tren.

Llegamos a Madrid por la parte
trasera, un desmadre con los
primeros rayos del sol, como
oro vaporizado, masticado
y en pedazos.

A mí me faltaba cruzar el Atlántico
en un avión mucho más rápido que
Colón y con mejores intenciones.
Desde el Caribe le cantaré a las
dos horas que residí en Bobadilla.
brindaré un Olé a los teenagers
de Málaga su alegría como sanjuanera,
inventaré flores para las moras
de Hay Salam,
tantas gazelas y aves que de momento
aterrizan en los árboles de panas
por la carretera de mi pueblo
un olor a África con tanto sueño.

POEMA CHICANO

Los Angeles de mi Chihuahua Mama
Su carrucho de burgundy.
Ciudad que empieza y no acaba
Hay más calles que estrellas.
José Montoya poeta de Sacras-Califas,
El del Royal Chicano Air Force-
El del Highway 99
El higuey-
El de aquellas ese
De la balada ranchera
Lo dijo bien:
"Los Angeles es un desmadre, una pinche perdida allí y te
Lleva la chingada."

Rucas de amanecer-mole poblano-chile verde besos
La china poblana-sarape panries-jalapeño miradas
Las Lupitas que salsita down Pico Avenue
Que crucigrama con Sunset Boulevard
Más largo que Cuba,
Sus malinches lenguas de la poesía
El guachupín Cortez padre de las voladas
Bilingües.

L.A. del cielo químico
Se vive en el carro—
Se pasan paredes de murales aztecas
Máscaras de Chichimecas ojos
Cachetes yaquis enchinaos
Harina de maíz en metate de colores
Sueños de mescal—por sorpresas
De Olivera Street—ciudad en medio
De un desierto.
Maravilla Housing Projects
Vatos locos
Pandilleros, cocos pelaos
Tatuajes como is fueran
Lienzos para Frida Kahlo.
Homegirls rucas

Bonitas doncellas con el
Tatuaje de la cruz azul
En sus manos—
Hablan palomitas de caló
Al lado de carruchos
Pintados como is fuesen
Pirámides—
Olor de carnitas y frijoles
Bajan en alas de águilas.
Desde las ventanas
El acappella de los oldies
El Little Joe y la Familia.

Ahora en esta antillana isla
Me recuerdo tus panes dulces—
Y tus picantes Serranos.
Aquel East Los
Infinito Barrio
Echo Park
Frogtown
El Mercado
Como is estuvieses en México
Grande como liga de fútbol
Mariachi por todo aire—
Braceros con sus botas de cuero
Tequilazos de Simón ese,
Bigotes que llegavan a la frontera—
Su español volado tejiendo
Por aquéllos otros Chicanos
Más pachucados pochos
Creando un tráfico de polka
Y emplumado mescalito hip-hop
Por todo el San Bernardino.

Órale, pues—
A la chingada el español
Y el inglés:
"Hey vato, where's Chuey ese."
"Está en la chante con su ruca, trais fralo, dame trola.
Buena yeska—Tijuana mama—tus ojos llegan a Jalisco,
Jalisquéate ya."

Virgen Guadalupeña—Ponte trucha
Por todo Aztlán
Estrella Mística.

La Virgen como tatuaje
En la espalda de aquél
Que le dicen el Chino—
El que era pinto
Allá en Soledad
También en San Quin—
El más chingón
Carnal del Fredy Mejías
De Santa Ana
Llegaba como la breeza.
Se conocieron en la pinta,
Estaba todo el East Side
Y el Valley también
Hijos de Pachucos
Generaciones de low riders
Esa vena que se va por Arizona
En el Interstate 10
Y llega a Albuquerque
Nuevo México—
Las Sandía Mountains
Huevos rancheros
Las Cruces
Llano Quemado—
Ojo Caliente
El Río Grande gorge
Mirar pa'abajo
Es ver el infierno—
Esos páramos de Juan Rulfo
En el norte
Mariachi y turquesa
Pueblo Taos ancestro collares—
Huercas con ojos de pura plata
Llenos del firmamento Oaxaca
Como oyen todo el metote
Las sultanas—
Oigo los caracoles danzantes

De Andrés Segura—
La fragancia del copal
El órale pues—los híjoles
Descienden por la montaña
Borincana de Jagüeyes.

El Californow de retratos
Los zoot suits
Sombreros de aquéllas
Estás qualifi—
Saludos Juan Felipe Herrera
". . . show me the way to San José"
Y tus cantos de paya papaya va paya.
Alejandro Murguía y las perdidas
Que nos dimos buscando a la tamalera
Callejera y la tortillera casera—
Y el Alurista que se inventó Aztlán
De la mitología—
Como cruzábamos la frontera—
Empezabamos en Chicano Park / San Diego
Y llegabamos pistiando hasta Ensenada
Casi sin feria
Donde en la playa
Taquitos de sesos y madres—
Aquel viejo que dijo:
"Ponle limón a todo para evitar
La cruda de estas son las mañanitas."

Ah, California, mi segundo país
Hoy suenas con el Suavecito de Malo
Y el jingo pop de Santana.
Y los bellos terremotos
Porque allí hasta la misma
Tierra bailaba.
California el poppy de oro,
Rascacielos de redwoods
Califorica
Californow
Califas
C/S
Con Safos.

from

panoramas

1997

Paisaje que no pasa nunca:
cierro los ojos y lo veo.
—Xavier Villaurrutia

Now as reality is such as we have
affirmed, that thou art imagination
and that all thou pierce and that
thou doth designate 'as other than
me' is imagination; for all existence
is imagination within imagination.
—Ibn 'Arabi

The Lower East Side of Manhattan

By the East River
of Manhattan Island
Where once the Iroquois
canoed in style—
A clear liquid
caressing another name
for rock,
Now the jumping
Stretch of Avenue D
housing projects
Where Ricans and Afros
Johnny Pacheco / Wilson Pickett
The portable radio night—
Across the Domino sugar
Neon lights of the Brooklyn shore

Window carnival of
megalopolis lights
From Houston Street
Twenty kids take off
On summer bikes
Across the Williamsburg
Bridge
Their hair flying
With bodega bean protein
Below the working class
jumping like frogs—
Parrots with new raincoats
swinging canes of bamboo
Like third legs
Down diddy-bop 6th Street
of the roaring Dragons
Strollers of cool flow

When winter comes they fly
In capes down Delancey
Past the bites of pastrami

Sandwiches in Katz's
Marching through red bricks
aglow dragging hind leg
Swinging arms
Defying in simalcas

Hebrew prayers inside
metallic containers
Rolled into walls
Tenement relic
Roofs of pigeon airports

Horse-driven carts
arrive with the morning
Slicing through venetian
blinds
Along with a Polish English
Barking peaches and melons
Later the ice man a-cometh
Selling his hard water
cut into blocks
The afternoon a metallic
slide intercourses buildings
Which start to swallow
coals down their basement
Mouths.

Where did the mountains go
The immigrants ask
The place where houses
and objects went back
Into history which guided
Them into nature

Entering the roots of plants
The molasses of fruit
To become eternal again,
Now the plaster of Paris
Are the ears of the walls
The first utterances in Spanish
Recall what was left behind.

People kept arriving
as the cane fields dried
Flying bushes from another
planet
Which had a pineapple for
a moon
Vegetables and tree bark
popping out of luggage
The singers of lament
into the soul of Jacob Riis
Where the prayers Santa Maria
Through remaining fibers
of the Torah
Eldridge Street lelolai
A Spanish never before seen
Inside gypsies.
Once Cordova the cabala
Haberdasheries of Orchard Street
Hecklers riddling bargains
Like in gone bazaars of
Some Warsaw ghetto.

Upward into the economy
Migration continues—
Out of the workers' quarters
Pieces of accents
On the ascending escalator.

The red Avenue B bus
disappearing down the
Needle holes of the garment
factories—
The drain of a city
The final sewers
Where the waste became antique
The icy winds
Of the river's edge
Stinging lower Broadway
As hot dogs
Sauerkraut and all

Gush down the pipes
of Canal

After Forsyth Park
is the beginning of Italy
Florence inside Mott
Street windows—
Palermo eyes of Angie
Flipping the big
hole of a 45 record
The Duprees dusting
Like white sugar onto
Fluffed dough—
Crisscrossing
The fire escapes
To arrive at Lourdes'
railroad flat
With knishes
she threw next to
Red beans.

Broome Street Hasidics
with Martian fur hats
With those ultimatum brims
Puerto Ricans supporting
pra-pras
Atop faces with features
Thrown out of some bag
Of universal race stew—
Mississippi rural slang
With Avenue D park view
All in exile from broken
Souths
The horses the cows the
chickens
The daisies of the rural
road
All past tense in the urbanity
that remembers
The pace of mountains
The moods of the fields.

From the guayaba bushels
outside of a town
With an Arowak name
I hear the flute shells
With the I that saw
Andalusian boats
Wash up on the beach
To distribute Moorish
eyes.

The Lower East Side
was faster than the speed
Of light
A tornado of bricks
and fire escapes
In which you had to grab
on to something or take
Off with the wayward winds—

The proletariat stoop voices
Took off like Spauldine
rubber balls
Hit by blue broomsticks
on 12th Street—
Wintertime summertime
Seasons of hallways and roofs
Between pachanga and doo-wop
A generation left
The screaming streets of
passage
Gone from the temporary
station of desire and disaster

I knew Anthony's
and Carmen
Butchy
Little Man
Eddie
Andrew
Tiny

Pichon
Vigo
Wandy
Juanito
Where are they?
The windows sucked them up
The pavement had mouths that
ate them
Urban vanishment
Illusion
I too
Henry Roth
"Call It Sleep."

It's Miller Time

I work for the CIA
They pay me with cocaine
and white Miami sports
Jackets
Free tickets to San Juan
Where I make contact
with a certain
Official at the Chase
Manhattan Bank

My contact, a guy named
Pete, asks if I know other
dialects of Spanish
"Can you sound Salvadoran"
They give me pamphlets
along with pornographic mags
They got their hands in the
backdoors of warehouses
If I want a stereo or a CD
That if a VCR
They could bring it all
at half price
Tickets to rock and roll
concerts
Where they drug the people
with lights.

The last assignment
I had was to contact
the PR division
Of a beer company—
Because for U.S. "Hispanics"
it was Miller Time
I contacted the brewery
A certain Miguel Gone-say-less
Invited me to lunch
That to meet him at La Fuente

Plush frijoles
Girls in peasant blouses
serving—
Low-key mariachi birdly
Community program directors
dining their secretaries
Big ol' bubble of tie knots.
At a back table there he
was
Drinking Dos Equis
and cracklin' tortilla chips
With him was a Camden, New Jersey,
Cuban who was going through
Town en route to Los Angeles
The lunch was on them—
Señor Gone-say-less
Had credit cards thickly
He had more plastic than Woolworth's.

They mentioned that the
beer company wanted to sponsor
Salsa dances within the community
Bring in the top commercial
orchestras
. . . and that while this dance was
Going on they wanted to pass
a petition against u.s. involvement
in Central America—
They demonstrated the form of some
organization they invented
Latinos Against Intervention
The petition had space for
the name and address of the
signers
A great list to have and share
among all government agencies.

They gave me a bag with three
thousand dollars in it—
It was my responsibility to

organize the petition circulation.
The Cuban guy tapped me on the
shoulder and said:
"Don't have any of the mixed drinks.
The bartenders at the dance are
working for us. The chemical people
are experimenting the effects of
a new liquid. Just drink the beer."

The festive event was smashing
people were stuffed into a ballroom
The band smoked
The beer company gave out caps
Ladies dressed like Zsa Zsa Gabor
Romeos thrown back propped for image
Circling the ice of their margaritas—
A full moon gleamed into downtown.

Next week the CIA
is flying me back to the
Caribbean
where I will assist in staging
One of the strangest events in
world history,
According to the description we
are going to pull off a mock
Rising of land from beneath
the Caribbean
Which the media will quickly
identify with Atlantis—
Circular buildings made of crystals
are being constructed in Texas
They will be part of the
Espectáculo
Which will have the planet
spellbound
Simultaneous with this event
the Marines will invade the
Countries of Nicaragua and
El Salvador from bases in Puerto Rico.

It will be a month of salsa fests
in San Francisco
An astounding mystical event off
Bimini
The price of cocaine coming through
Miami will drop
Everybody stunned party and
celestial
Glittering frozen and drunk
Circuits jammed with junk and
Information

In a daze of rapid commercial
flight
Colonialism and business
Mark their 500th anniversary
the world is free:
It's Miller Time.

Signed: Double Agent El Lagarto

MESA BLANCA

If I were writing on rock,
It would be the wind of the year
That caressing me will make
Me aware of the shadows on
A distant stone—
That signifies an eclipse
On some unseen distant roof,
From where in the form of
A kite a diamond leaves for heaven.

It would be that sound that I would
Make into a face,
Present it at the banquet of those
Who came lost on the boats
Punctuate on key
A coco-net of cybernetic eyes
Transmitting from the beach.

The sea a rush or mists,
Christ carrying the cross of Castile
Soldiers laundering heads of crushed guava
Have popped out of there
Salty like bacalao which here has been
Fricasseed with calabaza,
So we have to church the word
Mestizo
Half and Half—
So that textbooks claiming total
Taino vanishment
Should four pages later erase
The word *Mestizo,*
With the same mouth they say we are,
Was Webster wasting his time:
"mes-tiz-o [Sp, fr. *mestizo,* mixed, fr. LL *mixticius*]
a person of mixed blood; *specif:* a person of mixed
European and American Indian ancestry."

The sensational things coming together,
Of the Arawak-Taino
The only thing that remains is
What is not gone:
The looks,
The gestures,
The thoughts,
The dreams,
The intuitions,
The memories,
The names of fruits,
Rivers,
The names of towns,
Vegetables,
Certain fish,
The gourd making music
In the mountain,
The maraca making feet
Areyto dance,
And this cigar between my fingers.
More than half is the ground itself
The rock in my hands was in Arecibo's palm.
This is not to disagree with the
Anthropologists of text
But merely to reaffirm what they mean
When they don't say.

This paper which was a tree
Is crying for its leaves
That's the route of your mind
To dance its branches,
For that canopy red flower
Of the Antilles,
So high up in air spirit,
Flowing right through that bark,
A water shaft,
A city of bamboos
Liquefied fructus,
Humid swamp for that
Night frog,

To sing without rest
Till the roosters brush their
Beaks with the first
Arriving morning light.

The joyful noise of the night
What might be coming from lips,
Or the rubbing of legs
The full harmonic tropical berserk
Begging for love
In abundance
Not one thousand
But one thousand and one
Lights of cucubanos,
Morse-coding lovers,
That come down,
Meow not now
Of the cats—

For that's the flavor,
Within the opening of the
Two mountains,
A glance following the
River
That goes to fish its memories,
Scratched one next to the other
Like the grooves of shells,

To think that no one believes
We are here.
The past in the smoke of the cigar,
Bringing the future in-formation.

*

If a kiss left the mental dimension,
Entering the bone of dance hall,
My ears will reclaim the sound
Of your intended love.

Mostly it would be lost.
Both the poetry and the music
But to this side of things only,
'Cause flashing in the joy
Is the lord of the station,
So immediate as to almost
Be your tongue,
The salivic pointed,
When it truths together,
That moment when decisions are over,
And the motion is the only thought
Accomplished I hear the buttons
Slipping through the grooves of
Your fingertips
Out through the ether of the
Hole slice,
Now the back opens
As onto a land
Curving into a cave,
Most a moist is there—
That even fries lips
Which when the language dissolves
Gets hot enough to eat.
And it is always like this.
And it is only like this.
Ah Ha.

*

You were definite perfume
Aroma of incense that became voice,
Waving pink and blue plastic curtains,
Designs of Greek pillars
Contrasting with a wooden mountain house,
You left in criollo curls
And in the little tails of a glance—
I saw you in a Ford Granada
A silver metal moving like a star
Through the Catalan balconies—
You left in March

Through a rain forest
And came out in Ponce
Inside little bottles of water.

Children in the playa
Rubbing them with their coconut palms—
Floated you out as a giant head
Over the plena tambourines
The desert turban
Folding onto the rhythms—
Made on the backs of goats—
Riding them from the Caribbean
To the Atlantic
The crescent of the isle—
Descending through Sumidero
Once again the fragrance—
It became sound in the plaza
That swayed hamacas
Between the backstairs of the eye
And the windows of the nose—
Producing the melodies of an image—
Evidently.

*

The caciques were descendants of hydrogen
The sun hung upon their chest
Candles near the Indian Head
Simaron rockets
They passed singing through
Maví trees and rock—
They migrate with the blood
And filter through the bricks
Going toward feathers—
In the frozen ice a gold head
Ring upon a finger calls
And the water boils as if
For tea star anise—
When the prayer takes cadence
Someone's hands circle in the

Rising heat
Elevating from the intestines
A stream
Canoes in fierce paddle
Passing the throat
Broadcasting splinters of words
Like a prairie fire
En route to ignite the Crown.

*

A brush of airs full of words—
Ink on limestone marble—
The house itself is a poem,
Enter through the word: See
Shadows and rhythmic stone.
Sara churns 2,000 pieces of silk,
Passports for sailors,
Shepherd streams in the desert,
A caravana of gold tooth wagons,
Long skirts and sharp eyes.
A-string vibes in the air
The ear that heard the doors
Of the Cathedral of Burgos open:
Arco de Santa María—
El Cid and his sword
Pointed on the parchment—
Riding the sweet eyes of a little girl
Into the stare of macabre machos
Thirsty for blood.
Peace and rage
The picture brings memory to its knees.
The stroll of a scroll pulled
From the pocket of a Cataluña Street.
In the presence of the past—
Coming back to wonder
How a fresh of air
Can come and bow amongst us—
In the humid Antillean—
From dream to terror:

From Bohíos to apartments
From cathedral to mosque
Words ironed into stone.

The Castilians were coming
Out of the mouth of a volcano
Falling as ash unto red dirt.
Orocovis navel earthenware—
Artisans of finger palms
Had designs for each fruit taste
It is that subtle of a music
What silence for cadence split
Coffee people to enter you
Tobacco people to enter you
Sugar cane to enter you.
Corozo palms supply the material
For the black asabache
The space between stars
To enroll your finger
Vegetable craft
Working bones
Placing mother-of-pearl
Like light into the seeds
Three years before Columbus
The future spoke
The mouth of Volcanos:
Ashes.

*

Sprinkled all over the distance
Was the gossip that I'd been
Seen inside of a can
Thrown on the side of a road
Leading toward the songs of Ramito—
With a straw hat of fine stitching
At the same moment that
I was observing
A double-nothing
Lock a game of dominos

Closer down to the plaza
In the lime of El Zaragoza—
With the Ivory locked in hands
The matter was this—
What began with double sixes
Went into six trios
That ended in two fours—
Which was all the calculus
Don Felo needed to know
It was all going toward nothing—
So he held on to the empty frames
The counting fell precisely
'Cause outside a woman was calling
A girl named Cucha—
A man who knew twice the nothing
Rang: "That's the one."
When a player slammed down
One with four
To which the next one
Put four with blank—
Don Felo, who held the chucha
As Cucha walked by,
He saw the beginning of the end
Since everyone else had shot
Their blanks—
That's how it was possible
To highlight the night
Without leaving the can
Iluminiam of literature.
That's how the rumor spread
Into the arena
Of popular especulación.

That's why even when it's nothing
La chucha is everything.

*

What is the melody in the mountains,
Tubors imagining deep in dirt,

Used to be chanted rosaries
A cadence emerging out of wood,
Down ravine circling region
Eating the wide silence—
In trance with the rosary beads
A medieval gloss,
They lived in María's womb.

The coast what it got—
Rhythm and waves—
Palms clapping awake the perfume
Humid women in plaza dance
Tongues out of mouth
At the men who jump in the shadows
Panama hats transmitting
Toward the radar
Of the waist.

Cucarachas in the chicken dance
The roosters bebop.

Heat that sweat is the ink
A calor in Spanish that
The Church starts to run
Down Avenida Piel de Canela.

Hot waters rising through the
Songs of minerals
As mountain and coast
Morel Campos danza—
Antique contraband bones,
Flesh of bamboo walking
Senegal the Force Feet
of the mountain trovador
Rhythm golden bird
Inventing itself on the
Spot.

A disjoint of bone
Like yoga

The Rig Veda becomes
Foot and step—
From Guayama the priest
Ferment of herbs
Frog breath
Lizard Tail
Opticals of owls
And all the fires there are.

What choice do you have:
Might as well jump toward
land like seed
Tongue in moisture
With green mountain light
And coastal curves—
To lick the invisible
Generations.

Panoramas

The flora
Looked like books shelved
Out on the horizon and available.

Jobos of guanavana poetry,
Madrigals of papaya,
Haikus of lime
In perfect time
Through abundant roots
Of passion fruits—
Next to breadfruit encyclopedias—
Greeting the air
Before it lectures
Those who chance through window
A lustful invitation—
Moisture yellowing pages—
Verbal white birds flapping
Into the chapters.
Beaks that verse the prose.
The camp position invaded
By insects—
Biting the history that lurks
In caverns
Known to the reptiles of research,
And written in the Sunrise of roosters.

* * *

The river flowing through the sound: Guaraguao
Before the buildings rose,
A mouth singing vegetables
The coast as always
Receiving fire power,
The turn of the screw,
A screw in the fruit,
A mouth changing with the taste,
Where the sweetness turns sour.

Now the current is flowing without the view.
A past tense grows in the absent terrain.
As if language lived without our mouths to express it,
Little bottles of paint for the brush of rhythms.

Tiempo chasing tempos,
A string takes a siesta
Inside a maraca gourd,
Geo-swing instrumental trade,
The music of history
Below and above swords and cannons
The truth of the melody guarachin.

Walking from Africa
Camel of olive eyes,
A finger plays its neck,
A charm that can walk through
A palace displacing Roses.
Infinity of stars falling
Running through Yoruba sandglass
A Northern impulsion
Palm oil across metallic wire.

The Rock of Gibraltar motions
To write ballads around the
Belly button of Granada maidens,
The guitar a replica of her waist,
Castanets rain up into the
Stars that come out at day.

From the caves songs flying
Out like bats,
Language like sauce drumming
The streets.
Lips that visual.
Eyes that speak.
Painters mandala the eyes
Of Magdalena,
The father of Christ
A geometric sensation
Invisible like the love affair
With María.

Across vast liquid—
Taino classics
Filtering counsel out of seashells.
Tapping entities asleep in trees,
Inside rocks.
Gold and feathers
Brushing the guiros,
As they guide the legs
Through continental-island shifts,
Give us our daily cassava,
A thought of sky
Where the books are birds,
Inventing impressionism.

Messengers from the Sun
Drinking pineapple wine,
Agueybaná knew by heart
Memory 300 songs
And the names of his thirteen wives,
His forehead the wood
For ultraviolet solar etching.

The stomach of turtles
Adorn the pots,
The power of the wind
A drawing on your chest.

Skin music
Migrating to the point
Of a shoe
Tito Puente shifts
Dividing the edge of a razor in half.

Landing into squares and rectangles
The bronze incarnation,
The wings of history
In a glance
That will give birth
To travel once again
The caterpillar makes itself a dress.

* * *

What is in the night for you,
Pure heavenly China gardenia scream,
Sideways the machete a reflecting mirror,
As so sharp and astute the flower pictures,
Molasses: Cuts you in half.

Collapsing like moths into light,
The skirts lifting with the eyelid,
Avocados falling ass first,
Can you imagine a coconut
Lands smack into a mamey,
It's the cause of the night,
What is in the water bowl
Creating electrical flashes,
Possession moving the whole sense,
Through this forest of legs walking in events,
Flickering like a want,
Wondering what is that hanging in the
Trees, bananas or fish?

And just when you are really tranquil
The shadow of a fragrance crawls up the wrist,
The Antillean curve melody,
A production of dresses
The offspring of 19th-century agriculture,
Pre-industrial statues chewing fruit divine,
When they made a festival out of barbwire soup:
And survived—
How delightful can misery be
When forgotten?
Holding the breath of a hurricane
Those who survived are happy
With their scars.

Lightning wakes you up
To notice a lion in the room,
Reach for the machete in the mirror,
The beast's eyes are made of roses,
A wink and you're dead,
Nostalgia of frying yucca,
A white hat eating shades of green,
Taking the head off,
Palms dancing above tambourines,
Clearing
The retina of an owl
Throwing fire into the dark pages
That turn, turning the sky.

What disappeared appears,
It never left,
Aligning the rocks to the sun,
Threw my ear to the ground
Listening to the footsteps of
Turtles that passed
A millennium ago.

Ponce mulata waist that
Runs the waves,
Writing out of see,
Marking

With the cosmic point of feet,
The shoulders,
The tongue,
Navigating
A caligrafía of the cavernous night,
Pictographs edging off the stone,
A penmanship coming out of the bay
Like a moon glow.

Don't ever sleep again.

* * *

The horizontal song disappears into a
Cane of heavens,
Walking up cement and cal
Frosting sheets of zinc.
Ears are fingers
The night transmitting
The mountain pueblo
Gathering speed
Forming into a rock
Inventing the commercial jumps
The economic leaps
A cod fritter for two cents
Frozen in recollection.
There are those who well
Have deceived themselves
Splashly out of awareness
Into a dim of shadows
That the senses barely
Transport as they march
To the ongoing church
Satana never lacks friends,
It's in the swiftness of their walk,
It's in how fast their faces came
And have gone,
In locomotion losing

The capacity to designate
A drum into stories,
Well-spoken momentos
A voice into a tale
To send charm
Where there is a drought of love.

Sharp knives that sting the air
To death
Noise into the tenderest ears
That will melody to the next
Generation,
Each time the same persons
Start the same Journey
As if an endless standing still.

Your thought can leave from
The corners of the tobacco
Café Molased street
And pierce the length of the planets.
If at least one staff
Steps on its note:
Celebrate
'Cause those two ears come together
To make the shape of a heart
Listening
Above the rain forest.

* * *

Ambitious rains of moist September
The petal and the thorn bathing,
Mammoth love flowers,
Orchids
Covering with a fingernail the sky,
Diminishing trees and mountains,
Breaking into smaller pieces
Feeding the mouth of a guitar,

Strings of vines,
A neolithic chant
Manitas de Platas
Caves.

Argologo of bones
Skull thunder
Maria Clay
Play India
Rivers gone to air,
A moon of glass
Reflections
Guayaba tune taste
Flower flight
Rhythm sight.

Hands which were eyes,
In the wrist of maracas,
A necklace was a dress,
The embroidery of Andalusia
Captured sound of castanets,
Landscape opened like a fan
Encouraging rivers of tears.

Love which was before the
Bodies were born,
Breaking in the waves,
Having not yet arrived
To this mountain isolation.

Out in the maze in the minerals,
In the trees that will become beats,
The song will finally come to you
In a gulp of corn,
Birds' (Guaraguao) view
Of some cathedral mountain inside.
Steeples made of azucenas
Garza wings white:
Let it rain.
Monet brushing the breasts of Cayey.

*

Wait till you see Venus on her knees.
You will forgive the tongue-lashing
As nothing,
A kiss into the firmament
Between papaya and jobos
Light beams of the higuera moon
Each mile is a thrown hip
Till you exact the Dipper,
Charging seeds in the waist,
The voltage of a buckle.

The watts of Quike y Tomas
Explains the absence,
If it left one day,
Desire circles back
Till once again you are
A plaza glance.

*

Red ochre on your ass—
In the mountains
Gods whose names
Have been forgotten
Or mispronounced in Castilian.
Letters don't sound like trees
Voices barking bark
Lip to lip
Ceiba landwhich.

*

Conversation reaching the timing
When at precision: Two are gone.
A plumage of eyes begins:
Her hands lifting a white cloud
The shape of a calabaza,
In the limestone of caves

Naked in banana leaves,
With all the shells
That survived the Ice Age,
Putting into the same maracas
Seeds,
A jumping toad on her feet
A word to think of is: *Pana-Rana.*

*

Fertility locked in rock.
You hear the river you cannot see.
Darker than closed eyes
In black night.

Succumb.
Without question:
Serve to be served.

*

The song is horizontal
For at least a day or two.
It has its length
Walking up a cane
Of years held by mahogany
Paws
The fan of ether
That used to mold stone.

Faces speed against place,
In a hurry through the Panorama
Must be Satanas coming back
From doing one of his.

Are those the people who killed
Jesus in the church/again.
 Its capacity to nerves:
 A pitch of erotica
  Covered with clouds,

Tied in moño knots.
Swampy frogs jumping
The air of knives.

Huh, there's trouble in paradise
A drought of love
Stings the air.

This rush is in exile here.
I got a stress that won't translate.

In generations away
Each time the same
Journey
As if in an endless standing still.

The song has such length that
Soon you won't be in it.
The view we see
Belonged to another time
Other people upon it Mapayed.

And that if you heard it yet:
Right there build a shrine
'Cause if at least one staff
Steps on the note
The large night drops
Into the paint of Campeche.

*

No one here,
But me and the mountains.
The blue language
The soil wind,
Green bites.
Staring at the mountain
Till it grew a mouth to kiss,
Verdal suck.

*

Frozen flowers,
Dance when lightning hits.
On fire all the way to the water,
All flowers are temptation.
All dresses are made of flowers
All trees are tempted to fly
Into the sky,
A fragrance of control
Soils them in root.
One night a red angel
Dances the dandies flute,
Flowers reach coconut juice
To drink.
The outlet found:
They say, ah, keep it there
Keep it there.
Keep it there.

*

Wet black hair
When light tickles
The entrails of the night.
The flame receives a cool
Breeze from the maze.
Where are the singers from,
Where are the trumpeters going,
What are the drummers doing?

One member of the band disappears.
In the plaza the dance continues,
The crowd,
The salsa.
Gone:
The saddle, the trumpet,
And the horse.
That's 'cause everyone was staring
At the eclipse—
When closer by

There was a movement
Behind the lid of her eyes.

Conjunctures of the Caribbean,
The foot to the ankle in the sand,
Pumping salt out to the air,
Coconut is an innocent bystander
Which will assist in any shamelessness.
Now see how it slips
Now see how it shines,
After the trumpet
Came the timbales
Creating such a friction,
That had it not been for the rain,
The firemen would have arrived.

*

The index finger tracing turtle bellies,
Play clay sway pot in hut
For when the senses were coming to gone,
An imitation of a dream with juice,
That special cup of measuring moon,
Ceramic pottery miles below
The Christian skulls.

Flowers fruits vegetables
Not far a city kingdom arising—
The slaves and masters
Trying to live another game.

Pirates' ships on coastal riffs
Deeper yet loose mountaineers
Original copper
Spanish tramps
Painting Ollers olla
A new smell
With the pitirre birds
Lacing above the frame.

Other plains
Horsing through/
What can we say
How the root of the drum
Went like a white
Bird—
Dancing in coastal
Variations—
Pachangalandia
Of each and every
Curve of street.

Each place is hot
Each place is tough.
All plates have spice.

Caravan cumbia that left
Down Vallanata Bahía,
Planning plenas that
Merengue inside—
If each one of those
Movements
You strip to the bone—
Bomba
Cumbia
Rumba
Flamenco
Plena
Illuminating a cast of hips
In simalcas
A straw hat bopping through
White cement.

Art is motion standing still—
The furnace burning
The sparks of the sacrifice
Proceeding
Through the carnival
Fiestives.
History can do what it does,

Fire burns everywhere.

*

I dreamt that there were horses
Galloping upside down in the caves,
Stomping the guts of the mountains—
As the people stared into the blue
Wondering where all the thunder
Was coming from.

The same when the mare is in heat—
Get out of the way,
For horses have been known
To break a town to pieces,
Back when everything was wood.

Let a mare walk by at night,
Nightmare—
The stallion charges—
As if a force jumping
Out of hell.

*

There is a seashell
Coming through the air,
Creating a hiss that
Is now registering
in the candles of Brazil.
The earth will feel
The pulse of the wind
And a roar—
As if the ocean stood
Up in vertical fright.

People: Headaches
The radio telescopes
Can't find the frequency.

A seashell of beautiful
Surface whirlpool etchings.
Enclosing the ocean ballet.

Into eternity goes a grain
Of sand
All that the earth is
Inside a single groove
Of the shell.

*

Two times I saw you,
Two times dressed different you were,
So I called you once Anise,
And the second time Cocoa.

The first address you gave me
Was wrong,
Said you lived by the ocean,
Now you put it in the sierras,
Lost in the electric trees.
Both times it was you,
With different faces.
So nice you were made twice.
Choosing from those mountain ghosts,
Centuries by a flowing river,
Hiding from the historical process.
A love before words to speak
Before soil and lips,
A darkness of light speaking,
A mustache picking up the thunder,
Choosing the horizon flavor.

Now I wait for you to turn your face,
Before I call out your name,

Could be reptiles and horses
Climbing up your head.
Whatever
The changing moods of the
Lizard skin moon.
When we dance
Each turn a different mask.
A black berry,
The cinnamon bark,
An olive branch,
The mineral copper,
The falcon of the Berbers,
A Río Platense shine,
Your face inspiring
Local sonneteers/decimeros
It is within the crazy flora
Up all night taking pictures
With an owl
For the sun to develop them
In daylight.
The four faces took one
Picture Together.
Look now:
The salamander's face.

Some fish in reefs
Are like wet flowers.
Some went to give
The name of a fruit
To a neighborhood,
That's the barrio
Where I was born,
An Arawak fructification:
El Guanabano
Where I first saw
A version of you.
All around us
Whispering in rivers
And disguised as vegetation,
The pain of our language,

It knows the place we are,
But not who is speaking.

*

There is a printing
In the chance slaps and rustlings
Of the leaves.
Penmanship blowing in the wind.
Breeze that has traveled from afar,
Dipped ink in coastal salt,
Then went perfuming through
Mountains and valleys,
To circle a papaya,
Finally to gust through an open
Window
Where a body asleep
Sensates the momentary rush
The indoors of a Karmen,
Nothing could be fresher,
The sky avails itself in the house,
An air of desire,
A remembrance of
The flowered illusion,
Pano-ramas.

* * *

Comprehending the arrangement
Between the ingredients and the taste,
A going without knowing
Into each other
Of part and part
The conversation of silence
Timing of duality precise
As if you came into a forest
And turned into a leaf.

There is no salvation
For the burning invisible
A red statue
Dressed in a blue gown
Dripping out of a thought.

Accept what is walking
Graceful sky
Her hands lifting a white cloud.

Fingers rolling out of two palms
Held up toward the three tree palms
Whence the division jumps into
The same maraca
Frog feet following the dotting
Of the stars:
Succumb
Without question
Serve to be served.

No one here but me and the mountains
The paths full of bone and meat
Moving persons
Circling the aftermath
Of bombs
Which cleared
Their insides
Out—

Just the shape of the mountain
Is enough love
Speaking it writes
A resurrection of the tribes
Hidden in disguise—
If the wind blows right
And you are looking.

Atmospheric Phenomenon:
The Art of Hurricanes

Out of Africa arises a silence
To dance with the sky—
Spinning it makes its music in the air
Follows the route of the drum,
Comes toward the Atlantic—
To drink rum in the tropic islets
To use the bamboo as flute.

Big horizon of space upset,
Traveling through moisture and heat,
It has been known to throw steps
Of 200 miles per hour—
And yet a man of the mountains
Observed a miniature orchid
Purple and yellow
Hold on with such a pride
That it withstood the hurricane—
To hang with the Christmas flora,
Months later in our hot winter.

Each hurricane has its name
Its own character—
Hugo was strong and clumsy,
His strokes were like Van Gogh—
Bold and thick.
Pellets that were punches against the doors.
He came in vortex spirals.
Painting the sky of "Starry Night"
Above us.

He was poignant like tropical fruit.
Devouring mangos and guavas at will.
Breadfruit which flavors the tongues of Malaysia,
Enriching the waists of the hula dancers
In the South Pacific whose belly buttons
Hear better than ears.

Breadfruit which fries or boils
Was rolling through the streets
Of small towns surrounded by mountains—
As if Hugo did the favor
Of going shopping for us
With free delivery.

The Lesser and Greater Antilles like
Keys on a saxophone
An acoustic shoot
Each playing their note.
Did he blow?
A high sea note
Crescendo-waves
Coastal blues.
An air of leaves,
A percussion of branches
In the melody
The sound of green.

As if an asteroid fell
From the heavens—
Making all the religious
Churchgoers
Hallelujah onto their knees
To pray in total fright
In the face of death,
As if all that church attendance
Was not enough
To give them the blessings
When finally God sent
An ambassador in the form of a cyclone.

Makes one see that
People act contrary
To the laws of science.

Iris was a bitch—
She flirted from 14° north latitude
To 19° north—zigzagging

Lateral west
All that stripteasing
And she didn't come.
She went north,
Beautiful Iris
With her almond eye—
Full of lusty gusts.

Marilyn had curves—
A buttocky volition,
An axial memory that went down
To her tail.
At first she was a mere
Gyrating carousel on
The horizon—
On the satellite picture
She looked like a splattered
Sunny-side-up egg.
Her eye small
Like a black frijol
A beany socket,
Searching for the Virgin Islands.

Maelstrom of the sky—
A piranha of Carib moisture,
Calypso in the middle eye—
A vision which is also breath.

A hurricane is the heartburn of the sky—
A schizoid space,
A rotating mill of nervous air.
What made it so worried?
How did it become so angry?
The atmosphere sneezes.
God bless you.

A necklace of esmereldas,
The stairway of islands
We are sitting roosters
Waiting to be caressed

Our turquoise gown
Ripples in the wind.

Why was it that that Friday eve
When the hurricane was coming in
The beauty parlors were full?
Get dressed, María
Permanent your hair—
Luscious Caribee—
Extra starch
In case I hang my head out
To the breeze tonight.
Sand, palm, white rum
And perfume. A band
Of clouds for white shoes.

The islands look like spinach
That fell into a blender.
Whirlpool dancer
Licking the rim of the sun
Achieving the enlightenment
That comes through motion and moisture.

After Marilyn Saint Thomas
Was like a Jackson Pollock painting—
Telephone lines like a plate of spaghetti.
A canvas of pickup sticks
Covered with random-chance zinc roofsheets
Automatic rhythm art of happens improve—
A colorful square of inspiration.

Saint Croix was in the joy of Kandinsky's
Brush,
Lateral strokes pushing the sky
To collapse into molasses.

In the howling screech a thought:
Have the stars been blown away?

Caribbean islands
Sprinkled in the form
Of a crescent moon
Falling into Venezuela,
The land of Simón Bolívar,
The Orinoco
Currency of our blood.

A hurricane clears the earth's
Nasal passages
A hurricane would do Los Angeles some good—
The winds of Luis
Could have been packaged
In banana leaves,
Its eyeball of great
Cinematropic suggestion
Placed right outside Beverly Hills,
Driving through the freeways
Breaking the speed limit,
A vacuum of 100-mile radius
Dispelling contamination—
The picture in motion.

Tainos knew that palm Bohíos
Were portable homes—
When the tempest came
To remove them—
In two days they had them
Back up.

As the wind roars
Like a million ghosts—
Hurakán lingua accents each letter.
Going through in total disrespect
Of industry and technology
And conventional itinerary,
Things disappear.

Hurricanes go west
Then north to be cool.

A spirit which knocked
Down Antillean coconuts
Could still be breeze
Cooling tea in Scotland.
My dear Lord—
What passes through
A fruit of passion—
To sniff among the English.

The horizon was a bowl
For Marilyn to make her stew—
Stir in the escabeche
The ocean soup.
Ancient appearance
Would have been
Below in caves.
Subterranean Church
Next to the hidden river
Flowing in peace—
Allowing the passage
Of Hurakán—
Bowing in respect.

TIME ZONES

Time is crying upon the backs of lizards,
Through the white stone of the medieval city
They dash.
The houses that are walking up the stairs,
Flowers out of ruins,
Further into the fortress,
The sounds of a language registers
In our dreams.

Words which are my hat in the city,
Coming through the bamboo
The shadows of lost meaning—
Tilted light making slivers
Through the forest of the mambo
Behind the eyes.

Time will shine your head into skull
The circle song will come again and again,
If we forget how to lay out a village,
Just open a guayaba in half,
These seeds are perfect,
And can guide you back,
Your hands the electric of the ghosts.

In the Persia of shining alfombras,
A belly button silks upon a horse,
Enters a tent of rhythms,
Makes the trees dance into shape,
Rubén Darío saw them in the river,
Bathing in the echoes of the castles,
His Indio head,
Clean enough to measure
The tempo of a camel,
The first string that vibrated
The Rock of Gibraltar,
To sway Greco-Roman lips,
Arising fire of Gypsy song,

Was making Castile dress and undress,
With the sounds that were hitting the moon
And falling down unto earth as colors.

Of boats that were my shoes.
Atlantic chachachá.
Splicing through 101st Street brick.
Which covered dancing verdure green
Rectangular mangos,
Cylindric bananas
Sounds in the sky blue tropic: mind.

Trees are making maracas
That will soon make you dance.

Water is their god of cadence,
As I sea walk through coconut heights,
Legs of tamarind,
Purple orchids arranged like syllables,
Insects of the morning dew sting verses on café.
In embroidery of Italians,
Garcilaso came to José Martí,
Who ducked Spanish spies
In Manhattan
And hugged Walt Whitman's beard in Philadelphia
As the Cuban Habaneras' Shango
Made it south to tango.

Boats are ages sailing on water,
Parrots are flying out of castanets,
Flamenco peeling pineapples
That go up the river,
The water that became El Quijote's language,
As a cane field disappears into a bottle,
To awake in a little town
With molasses orbiting the cathedral,
A wooden saint slicing through the
Mountain full of potassium radiation,
Slanted plátanos pointing into medieval
Liturgy,

Bongo and ocean waves carving
Phantasmal antiquity
Through the fabulous language
That has taken the shape of
An Andalusian rhyming door,
One after the other.
Perfume pagano
Sailing out of the archways,
As Ricardo Ray turns into a centipede,
Marching across a Brooklyn piano,
For dancers to Sanskrit their
Gypsy feet,
Upon Albaicín ceramic tile.
Caribbean sun melts the caramel,
Making our first national flag:
White skirts waving in the air.
Machetes taking off like helicopters
Chopping off branches for timbale sticks,
The hands of the sun hitting the
Moon like a drum—
Making the atmosphere of moisture
Heat up,
For the chorus of the song
To come back down upon us polinizando
The carnival flower,
A serenade walkilipiando.

Sliding upon seashells,
That disappear into the foam of time,
One age living next to another,
We are both living things at once,
We are the cadaver that is
About to be born.

If You See Me in L.A. It's Because I'm Looking for the Airport

to John Daley and Lewis MacAdams

Even without Hollywood
It would still be an invention,
An imperialist drama from the
Spaniards to the Gringos,
Some automobile Hopalong Cassidy,
Arty hillbillies doing 90
On the San Bernardino
It's like a baker drops you
In the middle of the dough
Of the rising angel cake.

What is it, just a script in motion.
A performance,
Cameras rolling without text
So far through Sunset Boulevard to get
To an idea—
A Russian corner
A certain Gorky that salvaged beer.

What city,
A wiring of freeways, suburbos,
Only when you turn the TV on
The news convinces you that
There might be an attachment.

Billboards
So that perhaps if you're doing
Eighty you could look at them.

The relationship of people to
Their TV is a perversion
In the pocket of some
Beverly Hills cat pyschiatrist—
Lap cats forced to sit with

Owners dizzied from remote control.
Don't get me wrong:
There are great literary geniuses
Practicing dialogue for be-cool movies
Try reading that enviro/mental snarl
From a Caribbean balcony
Things people say down the street
In spontaneous coconut drops
Finds parking in the lot
Next to proverbs
And rhythms.
More than cheeseburgers
Gay or those that drive straight
Off Maliboo
Speed I can't get to,
I am deprived by distance,
A barbarism that Jajuyas
So far from Rome—
An immigrant eternity
Should that make it unique,
Is that a third of the planet
Outside the doors of San Juan.

L.A. is constant May Day
Residential barns
Off of constantly circulating
Traffic—
Wide enough so that you are
Not crowded by the slave
Quarters of looney tunes,
Utility living in mind,
Just keep the body running
Like a '57 Chevy.

Every ten years everything
Starts all over again.
If it were not for the oldies
What landmarks would there be?
The place would only have a future,
Nothing happening yet—

It's coming.
Can I park your car?
Can I take your order?

Car flirting
Car sex
Ah, if I get that chrome
What gets out of them
Diminishes.

I have fond memories of L.A.
Getting-lost stories on a pile,
The kind of off-the-track
Where you run out of gas
And can't find a gas station.

What would the Mexicans want
L.A. back for?
They got Mexico City
And can give lessons
On how to perfect
The pollution.

So if you have survived
The image of your own image—
Perhaps you see something
Walking outside your windshield,
A mural of Huichol geometros
Giant Mayas up on project walls,
A Guatemalan woman carrying
A bag balanced on her head down
Pico Street climbing some stairs
To a blue-coated apartment
Where Mayan corn
Hangs like framed saints.

A chanting that is old
In doo-wop radio,
The palms of the hands
Playing eternity upon

Tortilla flats,
A bridge over a river
That refuses to die
Linking what is not lost,
With what will not survive.

Now I see it in the rear
View mirror
La Virgen de Guadalupe
I gave my flowers to
Upon a wall
Like a gate into the East Side
A little brown boy and girl
Holding hands
Clutching tamales
As they walk toward Brooklyn
Of the urban Michoacán,
Now the ultra-new buildings
Are smaller
Than the shine of the
New World eyes
Beholding the distance
Of the smog.

seeds

1996-2000

Muhyi-din Ibn'Arabi

Born in Murcia-Spain not far from the sea,
salt in the wind always good for colors,
That day stars came down to become almonds,
frankincense-luban imported from Zafar
Circling breezes from the moon,
respiration expands across deserts,
lips of dates the sweetness of conception,
Revelation of hidden silver
shining from the interior of the earth.
Avicenna hovered as an angel,
moist sound opening above the roofs,
A purple spiderweb spread,
over a green of silence.
The planets divided into shoes,
sublime of the skies,
Arabi's hair detected floating ice
blue-turquoise repeating the verses
of the book.
Observing the content of the Breath,
eyes fresh from zodiacal towers.
Such visibility from the Bay of Cartagena,
where chocolate from the Indies melted,
Parrots escaped from the cages
they crossed the Atlantic in,
By then Ibn'Arabi was imagination,
and the local mosque desecrated
By the plaster of saints.
Writing text with an aerial
concentration the reader has to know
The letters in the polished mirror
of their own sight.
A perception that not all the
words find you awake,
Meaning trembles uniting opposites,
syntheses of the bone structures,
Whereas people are in the flesh
fighting.

A turban above the head unrolls
if the syntax confuses the novice,
I am disguised as tone
to regain my throne,
The taste of nuggets,
cream of walnut,
The study of Café,
the heart opened
To the thoughts of Venus,
observing rhythms,
Before the adobe of the earth,
Adam coming down as a quill,
through the dawn of
The palms' antennas.

Ibn Rushd (Averroes) took
him through the caracol
Streets of Córdoba,
Through the laughter of
Marrakech exposing teeth
of Berber gold,
In Fez spirits of architecture,
ovals, corridors, shadows,
Fountains of water
cadence of the azulejos
Walls of poetic tiles.
In Mecca he found a harmonica
blowing through the sand dunes
of the solar divine
Into the symbolic earth,
he played it to produce
Her olive flesh
From which there is knowledge,
of itself to know itself,
Circulating the black stone
during the clarity of that white night.

The Concord Grapes below her eyebrows,
framed beams in the desert's museum,
Visible from the bottom of a Jupiter crater.

Though the earth is contaminated
Abu Bakr Muhammad ibn al-Arabi
saw another world,
Right here in this one before
his eyes.

Water which is on fire,
of all places and spaces
The same truth
"Fusus al-hikam"
A gardenia of iron.

In 1621 Murcia
there were women who
Would not let you sleep
through the marvelous
Memories
See them gyrating
I would kiss the ripples
created in the water
By the dipping of her ankles
in a lake,
Traveling through perfumes,
distinguish them all as prayer.

Nabokov

A nationality of language
spread on butterfly wings
Crossing borders
What puns can I feel of his
in the mulatto mountains
A fixed character
in a molded face
What other screw has to be tightened?
The Russian aristocracy . . .
a glimpse of a living room,
A portrait of a statesman,
a foreign joke
I translate into coconuts.

A pillar separate from sentiment,
to throw light on imagined truth,
Observing through tangles
the curve of the knots,
The compartments of botany.
A man of Russian rhymes
available to English phonetics,
Did he iron Pushkin's coat,
pulled it out from the inside
Translating the intent of the lining.

A foreign American writer
an old desk he never cared about
Upon which a magnifying glass
Read the mini Kandinsky
upon the Monarch's wings.

Just like the exile of art
from the current,
Studying bones
the flesh it needs upon it,
For architecture must know
of steel, beams, planks,

Mahogany and wind,
awareness of what jags out
From the smooth everyday
uniformity.
A selection of events
so that they feed necessity,
Leaving chance to those
who arithmetic a future
Doomed with Paradise.

Economic levels
are not towers of observation
From the top to the bottom
avatars have song.
Blindness in Count Marmalade's house,
a clear night of symbols
In the south Bronx.

Lolita A book about writing,
inside the Latino sound of her name,
Outside the piercing of a bud
Spanish-Capullo,
A manual of mechanics,
a directory of Who is not Who.
A liar who doesn't love
his own metaphoric heat,
Just look at her without
the previous prose on,
She stands up and jumps
out from the page to walk
again—the streets of her origin.

A passage of time,
or something that is ancient now,
Memories never lived,
Ada-ración
a motion passes by
We are notion
in the scripture
Of the citizen
of his words.

Juan Gris

Poem with Still Life

A circle/A shadow——with a square
Shade
Outside of which light wants to get in;
Dance in
As if forbidden there in the rectangle
To laugh——
Mechanical pencil makes itself
A door as to liberate guitar strings
Silent in the geometry of patterns
Wants to levitate with duende
Figuring a woman who is the spine
Of the la'ud
An arm traverses her hollow interior
of endless resonance
Plucking the center abyss
What's more, higher lines
Vertical
Crossing the horizontal
Cylindrical wrist
The sound then gives birth
To flowers
Marching into the circle
Flamenco in paint——
Without moving it exudes:
Each thing talks that
Each that talks thing.
Made up of a gathering of silence
"Harlequin with a Guitar"
Bolero cubes
Like ice in brandy
Transparent
Dimensional lament with joy
The third dimension of desire——
The shape of a door opens
Bluest sky.

In this realm
If you didn't go to church—
Just kneel
In front of:
"Seated Harlequin"
A pantomime captured
With spoken lines
The joke of life
Things just visible enough
To bring them back
From a dream.

CANTINFLAS

Montezuma's court jester
Quetzalcoatl's mime.
he is everything in us that laughs
The smallest bones
aligned with the verses of necessity
He walks upside down,
it's not his pants falling
It's a pyramid rising,
Coatlicue was at the formation,
Ollin movement gave his joints flex.

Even in terror I have seen
the charm of grace.
Lord of movement
dismantling the bourgeoisie,
A tortilla in its face.
Aztec counterculture
going up an elevator
In the squares of buildings
on la Avenida Reforma,
Cantinflas struts on
the shining marble floors,
His feet talking
the language of riddles,
The syntax—the grammar
arrive as if to rescue
The poet exiled from the
dictionary.

Sense sensulet,
Cantinflas is the only
man who doesn't
Have to move
to travel the cosmicos
Cómicos
Our mestizo jaws
go from grin to cracklin

Peeling in the spreading
and even then swelling.

Without motion
he makes murals of flowers
Jaguars and skulls
he pulls out of a clay pot.
Egyptian and Toltec theater,
alive of humanness humeros
Humoros
He gives Charlie Chaplin
the Americas conquered ridicule
Ridículos back
in a flaming heart of laughter
upon the altar of sacrifice,
For we were born for joy,
Cantinflas brings the teeth out,
to overcome the hacienda
Son of a bitch,
We are the earth
He takes for gyrations
orbits which expose the king,
one pivotal turn in any scene,
Spread feathers
Wind which strips
the Patron's tuxedo
Exposing us all
as cookies
In the shape of skeletons.

José Martí

His words were Bahías
or actual trees
Painted fish dancing around mangroves
(mangle=An arawak reincarnation)
As if in the air where Martí
Was born—Cubanacan—The East Trade Winds:
Circled adventure in the wordscape
of what comes together.
The Orishas separate the eyes
of the faces upon the Cataluña fan,
History was already a work of crochet
The volcano's lava simmering
In his habaneras swifts
The contredense of his steps.

Shackled at nineteen for poetic awareness
The inquisition on automat across
Atlantic
Swift upon the head
Aguazulie-Regla
The Kings whip lectured
Cuba/Puerto Rico
Spain's final stand
They finished where
they began
The isles of the Carib.

Martí lived on the pictures
of his memory
on the road—in movement
Like the verbs in his prose
Spinning like rumba orbits
Lifting the journalist maracas
Essay metaphor counter image
Explicit contra thought—Sonorous
Woke up a drowsy Spanish,
To the tune of something

is happening now.
Unamunu got the telegraph
As theater performance.
Pageantry of Saint Jolts,
San Meneo de Linguísta
Upon an altar of
Rows of burning wax.

Walking Manhattan's Lower West Side
Spanish spies through the cold.
Restful in the Catskill Mountains
Sights growing Palms.

Upon the shoulders of his struggles
His son's playful photos
Afloat in the always present
Distance of Cuba
Through the blizzard's white frost.

The manigua of his hurt,
Feeling transposed through harbors
Luggage made of straw units—
Eyeglasses of piercing beams
With slow ink waving Atlantic
Boats,
Memoirs of "The Girl from Guatemala"
Muses up at night
Their own burlesque of Third Avenue
Sprays:
"She died of love and nothing else."

Like Vallejo
He saw where wings became shoulders,
once he flew around
Rows of marble
Nymphs who came alive
Upon the kiss of words,
Like antillean woodpeckers
Carving women out of trees.

Blow song José,
Juan Tanamera
                    Guahira

At the end he went into his language
He performed his desires
Versed Simply
into Two Mouths River
Into the tropical sun
Bright and visible
Inviting the bullets
of the popular song

Guahira . . .
                    Juan Tanamera.

Jalalu'd-Din Rumi

Principle of the "Perfect Man" is creation,
for in what else could one know the self,
The something . . . the pearl,
mountains and trees are urges,
Desires once hidden
A river which we hear inside
flowing in Saturn.
What are these colors colors
which I can only perceive
As sound.

I found you when I had no head
no tongue
No eyes
yet I was looking straight
At your taste
like a position in memory.
Wondering through florescence,
swimming in lava,
Iron ore takes position
in the molten stew,
Litanies of sound,
I prostrate before music
and the rotations of a skirt.
Utilizing the fingers of my hands,
I navigate through the nebulous
regions.

It's all the same
a Buddhist monastery—
Gongs in the Himalayan morning,
vistas from Tibetan windows,
Mountains that travel with air,
sculpture of patience.
Meaurements of the Torah,
the weight of a judgment,
Or Maria mother of us all,

Monserate of basalt—
Babalu Aye
What patterns of drums
bring to light
                    tilt over
In the mambo.
The candles of Allan Kardec
the Frenchman
The cross and the glass of water
upon a white table cloth,
Ancestors come to dine
upon our nerve ends.

Rumi there are sea creatures
walking upon land
Bowing at Jazz churches
praising Monk.
Upon the Persian rug
of a red sunset—
Raises the voice
which is fire itself,
This place is in flames,
sparks are our bodies touching,
Throw yourself into the sound,
words which do not have things.
Dancers dressed in black and white
mulattos dancing upon bones,
Traveling toward the sun
cha-cha-chá of whirls,
Rumi already saw the Martians arrive
doing the dervish hop-around.

Balkh—a town I can only fountain,
white chalk rises to greet the clouds,
Its gardens suspended in eternity.
We are spinning around
one foot in Saturn
Another in Mars—
our heads (hallelujah) spiraling
into the sun—

Which finally eats us all up.

Poetry is stumbled upon
as if it enters,
We move into an area of
speaking air
It is typed upon our tongues
what "entes" arrives.
Rumi's scribes followed
like servants,
When the girls were musing
etchings upon papyrus
Witnesses of what can be deciphered
from starlight.

Like a circle
a cyclone of knees and arms
Aeronautics into the firmament.
When the rhythm starts
it is Rumi
Who first jumps into the flame.

La Lupe

Her voice comes out of her knees,
her fingernails are full of sound,
Birds are in her lungs,
which gives her gargantuan flight,
A florescence through ether waves,
like ancestral Morse codes.

Oriente province de Cuba
her first steps.
At nineteen she dismantled retinas—
roosters blew themselves inside out,
When she swayed by cathedrals they folded,
guayacan trees fell to their knees,
Mountains bowed with the contents
for ajiaco.
She filled the horizon with kerchiefs,
gypsies danced behind her,
Her bracelets were snakes,
forces were captured in her gold chains,
The moon was in her silver,
there were reptiles stationed
In her Afro-Siboney cheeks,
there were in her Asian eyes
Radars picking up the fingertips
of the piano player—
The language of the trumpet—
black changos landing upon
The shelf of her eyelids.

She motioned in songs to live them.
Her passion destroyed the container,
She blew up into false promises,
romantic lyrics tied her in knots,
Broken into pieces of kisses,
she knew it was "theater"
That you offered,
A landscape hanging in the

museums of desire,
Rows of guayava paste,
stories that according
To your point of view,
salons of dried roses.
Illusions.

Her songs became the windows
of the city,
In the distance a hurt bellows
from a bird locked in a radio.

Classroom teacher of tropical children,
reading to them native flora—
A wind entered her and she flew to
New York,
eating the skyline,
Bridges of electric lights,
conduits to the house of the Saints.
At the Jefferson Theater
she melted the microphone
Into liquid mercury,
and an ambulance had to
Get her off the stage.

She embodied in gowns, capes,
dresses, necklaces, bonnets,
Velvets, suedes, diamond-studded,
flowers, sequins,
All through which
she wanted to eat herself
She salvaged us all,
but took the radiation.
Each time she sang
she crossed the sea.
From the Bronx
she went back to Cuba,
Adrift on the sails
of a song.

MACHITO

What gourds that have had the privilege
when even something that passes by chance
is accommodated—
Is there a tree that would not uproot
itself in Cuba or Puerto Rico
To be the handles of the maracas in his palms?

As if competing with nature to integrate
fusing elements like a tropical forest—
An animation covering the horizon
a whole landscape in motion—
Arabian horses in single file
then dividing into threes and twos
As if following the two clave sticks
out of the Nubian desert
Into the Antilles of focused sun.

Luis Miranda master drummer
he heard the rhythms from above
His hands giving speech,
a dictionary of Timba which is Conga,
Under and above the rain shower (Cangana)
Mario Bauza directing the thunder—

Machito's song was tradition
piped in tongue exact,
A whole village moving in measure,
hopping over bridges of brass,
Shining through sheets of rhyme,
squeezing through tunnels of rhythm sections,
Cooking pigeon stew, throwing in jaw,
Spice of shells and light,
irony for Ogun
Fire for Shango.

His music brings a levity to the feet
puts doubt upon the law of gravity,

The Afro-Cuban's big band
Sparkling like rows of Champagne bottles
With Graciela
        "... ay José asi no es,
        ay José ponlo otra vez ..."
A peacock of feathers
brushed against mahogany.

As all birds know where to land,
Parker flew through the clave
designing around the pulp of mango
Batida
"Mango manque" Charlie blew blue
into the rumba
Machito's Manhattan
the buildings were maracas,
Bricks of Duke Ellington notes,
Gillespie could see the flavor
of black beans.

Within a mirage of skyscrapers
Machito appears in a film,
wearing a straw hat
Walking an Ox,
He shifted geographies,
while deep in the earth,
The rhythm
        bongo
Stays the same.

Benny More

His sombrero and his shoes
said it all,
But then there was his mouth.
Such journeys that birds take
across the Atlantic,
The lumber of a boat,
the stretch of skin,
Fill the moon up with rice,
let it light up as a maraca,
Phrasing through coco palms,
Clave hands brushing pink dresses.

It is 1957 and the night is blue,
the coast is everywhere
With no beginning or end,
a circular border of taste.
Cardenas sculpted curves into
obsidian rock,
Talking to Bantu ovals of Cuba's
chekeres.

For the Yambu where you don't inject,
but the guaguanco of the sea receives,
The gyrating pelvis of Yemaja.
Walking away toward sand dune hills,
heightened our splendor of the
Horseshoe beach,
aerial view of her blue dress,
Beach grapes dancing Babarabatiri,
Almendro trees like chanranga violins,
foam and fried red snapper,
Chillos in Spanish swimming,
lemon on the song,
Fingers dialing a phone,
the hands of who has manifested
to play drum from blood destiny—
The third guitar improvises

through the shouting of goats,
Now flowers growing out of cowhide,
now bubbles in between marble,
Perfume between the teeth of sharks,
limericks caressing gently the neck,
So close the guitar in your hands.
While it is not known
how we fell in love,
With Benny's sombrero making shadows
to the sides of the saxophones,
Nautilus like waves of mambo
dancing toward the river's currency.
We verse in his blend of Spanish-Arare,
simultaneously shoe tips point
Lifting pants and skirts.
We'd never know
what elements: anise and crimson lips
Of shouldered cinnamon spiraling
through fruits of bomb,
In jars of syrup floating
slow guajira,
Dissolving into cancion fatale,
when the trumpets make a space,
An air pocket in the melodious rotation,
octopuses start playing pianos,
Surfing backwards toward the base,
glimpsing through the acoustic shells,
A soprano operation,
cigar rollers laying down capes,
Producing smoke for dance,
legs of horse Arabica,
Scriptures on the floor,
in Tibet they would make
Mandalas out of the sand,
weave blankets with kisses
from Buddha's lips,
Enchanted figurines scaling
through atomic moisture,
Full now of sodium,
from the transmitting mike,

His mouth to the bush.
Sonnetting nets to lance out
to see the horizon alit with
Choreo layers, elbows, and shoulders,
rows of curved hips.
Cheeks which house the sound—
without sombrero or shoes—
All is now flowers
reaching for where sky meets
ocean and birds fly in jealous
delight—

Sing if you're going to sing.

FRANK SINATRA

The way moths relate to the dust
upon their wings
Just there let's say
weightless flower paper.
Walls of a Hoboken home,
the Romanesque lullabies,
A tongue of wine,
a worker of air,
He controlled the gates,
a numbers man of the wind,
A fascist of orchestration.
The great operators of Italy
sing along the river's edge of New Jersey.
Manhattan of wool and tweed,
rhapsody of radio hours.
Fabrications of industry doing the
locomotion, jaggedy, swift.
This song relax.
Serenity through the urban push.
1942—Hudson river
Volare seagulls
The Roosevelt
garter belts
Nylon stockings with black lines
silk panties
The Chrysler Building
when it was a new pyramid.
Sicilian garbage collectors
who sang ole blue eyes's songs
Through cold morning work.
A troubadour's language
of precise Swiss watches
A fruity baritone sails—
making passage through cymbals
Trombones, vibes, cellos—
a spacing as if the dance
Of the planets with the sun,

Everything moves that makes sound,
it's a God of timing Pythagoras ciphered,
Just the right amount of color
upon the rings of Saturn,
fulfilling the lungs for breath.
The Venus of a Neopolitan cancionero
above marble columns,
The tunes of he who now sings
through the light.

KOBAYASHI ISSA

His eyes were binoculars
small things
Had the fury of the cosmos.
A winter enters a molar
a mosquito drinks up the ocean,
Tiny particles—a fly's leg
hits the leaf like thunder,
The very moon a cherry
in a beggar's pocket
And if it downpours rain
horses all wet upon "chrysanthemum"
Who have no knowledge
of fragrance emanating
From the strokes of a brush—
her kimono full of fruit
Five fingers in her womb.

His father's best crop: Issa
of the renga chain mountains
Of Yataro—
I'll compose it through
his photos
Watch the light in the river
plum trees covered with snow,
A jade Buddha in a garden
toned in the frosty optics
Of an owl through which
a moth crosses out of nowhere
Towards the porcelain light
of a cat's teeth
That pierced through
the morning fog.
Issa heard insects with sour
throats.
In case of the flies
he always swung with pad.
Bedbugs ran out of the sky

the mat of the stars
Covered by the blanket
of the blue firmament.
He saw facial features scatter
in the sunrise
Noses and eyes charge
up trees insert themselves
In random animation,
and then look back at
How ridiculous everything is
scarecrows eating rice
Dogs asleep upon melons
The rich try to buy
the poetry they do not have
Snow turns to shit
they frame it as art.

Quiet . . . Issa has reincarnated
lives in Detroit
Passes by barrio
polished Mexican house
Through window
sees kids hit piñata
Looks like flower
coming apart
With las 'mañanitas'
all is flor y canto
The horizon smiles with Issa
everything else
Becomes stupid.

MARK TWAIN

> I don't want no better book
> than what your face is.
> —MARK TWAIN

Rivers are always poetry—
Williams's Passaic
Julia's Rio Grande
what is a boat but some ear
Half wet/half dry
sunken with the fish
And their design upon style
Twain was wood
language skidded like grain
Through him
a circus of the absurd
He flew on the trapeze
and it (ain't) wasn't
Even his fault
He was in the kitchen when
they dropped the eggs
From gossip to the scratch
of cricket legs
A long glance at tyranny—
And how we can escape it—
And yet it is hurt
which is invisible
And gives us vision
How serious the serious enemy
More serious than two cents of grits
Otherwise it would be a breath
sliced in half—
And catch it right
lest it run off
        and you pay
For the balance.

If a river
Or a street formed you
The sentiment of experience
The sharp edges of eyes
The evil that lurks in mansions.

The river itself starts talking
it makes its own structures
of straw hats and sweat
Links of slanted English
Steamboats that devour
our illusions
Is not that the devil's jawing
in the courthouse.

I book for the pleasures
of the South
Location of locust trees
in these pages which now
Are muddy waters—
Laughter is justice
And life itself writes it.

MILES DAVIS

to Quincy Troupe

I've only been to East St. Louis within
the poetry of Miles Davis
And the music of Quincy Troupe—
feels like a different dimension
Of winds and escapades
houses dancing in rows
With arms and hats
abandoned in joy
In one of its streets
a young boy blows into the wind
Sunken within his fingers
an alloy of copper and zinc,
Molten—where they make that
In the heart of the body,
underneath the flow of the
Mississippi,
the child walks through the lava
Meets his mineral
where time makes sound worship
Auditory Blues Temples
strung Osun Palaces,
Metals melt like chocolate
in Miles's hands brass turns
To rivers of amber
"Round 'Bout Midnight" is the color
of honey
          Clover sweet
The New York skyline in
crepuscular light then
A slow blue shadow
through Riverside Drive
1955—

(once observed a Phoenix reposed
on a roof ledge—77th Street West

late in the night "Stella by Starlight,"
memoirs of Heliopolis staring into
the diamond dots of brass chips
a motherfucker who bertrayed all
locations of species)

With Gil Evans's fingers
Miles floated through Spain
like a saint
Giving eyesight to Rodrigo
in "Concierto de Aranjuez"
A gallery opens up
in the Andalusian sky.
Vineyards of such burgundy
the sound permits us to taste
Strokes of muslim structures,
the Visigoth's decors,
Gypsy etcher, Sad hurt
spirit of lament
                    Galaxial blues,
through miles of geographic fingers
Such a boat
A Bitches Brew of naked majas
out of Goya's brush.

Quincy's language of scattering
chopped-up beat pulsations
In the sunshine of Miles's brass
reflections
East St. Louis
across from St. Louis Missouri
Where T.S. Eliot felt the line
breaks like storm waves
A bit too strong
"No, this ain't the land for me."

Too many Miles of Music
Too many trumpets at the gates
Miles of Miles.

Washington Irving

A place of birth is necessary
but where do you become,
If you leave the cold
the familiar shapes—
The labyrinth of New York,
a virgin the way he saw it—
Wearing knickers the bockers (brokers)
selling Masonic edifices
Did rich get, cement and
pavement—Knickerbocker
On Manhattan
with Amsterdam A-new,
History of the docks
the curve of the Hudson,
The explorer hoping for Beijing
somewhere beyond Harlem.
Rembrandt's people,
must've been those faces
Bacchanal upon the casseroles
banquet through oscuro/light.
Irving in the ink of Peter Stuyvesant
who became a Yorksman,
A new white rose for New York,
before the cement went vertical,
Boxed mountains.

Did Irving see the Alhambra
pop out of the Adirondacks,
or did the flow of the Hudson
carry the music of the la'ud—
Did Mahoma* divide
the Long Island Sound
Into octaves.
A fairy across the Atlantic
Sevilla de las Indias,

* Peace be upon him.

in Granada (the pomegranate)
Look well at the inside of the
tiles
He slept in the Palace of Lions
within the Alhambra
Its gardens, waterfalls,
fountains
In El Generalife
where the beautiful verses
Were kept
        A cup of café
awaken the embroidery of tales,
A fabric of looms,
taverns and balconies recited,
He spoke to the women
who knew how to keep swords
From piercing silk,
and put cocks to stupor,
While they vanished through
chambers.
Irving's ears heard the spoken,
The narrative's traffic
which "cuento" is to tell
The number the cuenta to
count the account,
It was the television
of the age,
What Moors gave the Goths
Latin tapas such delicacies,
all suspended for time within:
Tales of the Alhambra
From the sketches of a
traveler,
Who heard the geometry
of Islam,
And later saw Zaida
float down the Hudson
on a carabela
going toward Spanish Harlem.

CLARABEL THE CLOWN

Once for the first time
the one time
A television floated into
our apartment
And the new world
became more faces and places.
Out of that box
the world started to spin.
The passage of a child
it felt like green heat,
Airplane
gray cold
Geography at six years,
odor, touch, and colors.
The corners became different,
down the street
A clarity of edges
iron and steel,
No more palms
or papayas hanging
Like footballs,
a deep red in the hallway
Marble pillars,
brass mailboxes shining
like a song,
Stairs from which you saw
no mountains
Up above
a bigger country
With a smaller sky.
The way those things were
coming
You'd learn how to pronounce
a word
And couldn't find an object
to put it on—
So many contraptions

which had no sound.
The monster of the train,
a giant subterranean dinosaur,
It made a noise of speed
and bang around,
I expected tropical rivers
at the end of the IRT line
Bamboos folding and molding
into church archways
In the wild.
The lizards of the last
channel
Scurried into cement,
the cogui's song
Became snow.
At night I was attentive
to the new glacial age
Which I had entered into
through some flash of
a wand.

Clarabel the clown
made you sit still
Almost ready to
eat the television.
"It's howdy-doodie time"
Oué?
What happened to my
grandfather singing with
Guitars—
and trucks that passed
With hanging cane—
White birds
with long necks curved
Like question marks?

Clarabel the clown
had that horn
Which he squeezed
"O.K. kids . . ."

My ears fresh out of
the Spanish strained
Fua Fua
He blew the horn again,
then commercials of
Candy bars
chocolate dripping,
Cupcakes animated
through space,
Bazooka bubblegum bigger
than heads,
Some Castro Convertible
furniture store
A little girl bouncing
like a ball upon a
Mattress.
Later in deep night
I plotted going
inside that box of lights,
Cause that's where all
that chocolate was melting,
chiclets
and that little girl,
All up in there in those
tubes,
Go in through all those wires,
come out wearing Hopalong Cassidy's
Black hat,
blowing Clarabel the Clown's
Horn at Sky King
charge down Avenue D
On Lone Ranger's horse Silver.
Falling asleep:
dreams of immense tropical
Flora,
an ox I once saw,
A waterfall caressing
a mountain,
Mangos the size of
New York buildings

all the pipes turn
Into bamboo shoots.
In that time ago
which was once.

FEDERICO GARCÍA LORCA

In Europe there are streets of stone
where leather has become sound
Vanishing—audible
in the peninsula which exits
Into Africa
           Iberian doors
opening—closing   Archways
Shaped like guitars   Visigoth
kitsch colored stones.
The same street has been
another tongue
Which licks another epoch,
preserves the flavor of an accent
The roots of our hair—
wooden boats upon the waves
Of our blackness, Shadows
upon the fountains of poetic
Tiles of flowers
               In the echos
of the al-Hambra
A structure/a book of verse
each room a young wife,
Precious you are air
embracing the plastic
Coconut palms whispering
to the crescent moon
Wrapped in the singing
of a rooster all crawling
Toward the Sierra Nevada
like a matador toward
His love the bull,
as the water streams
Down to the house of Allah.

India in the black flamenco
pants dance the Sanskrit
Whistle flute windows
of Albaicin rum—

Your presence under the
towers of the Mosque
Laura—Fernando
Salsa spins under the moon
stabbed by a cross
As we dance with your blood
our pierced Guarani ears
Naked islands—
Lorca in Cuba of rumba,
we are all gypsies of contraband
Finally America—an error in phonetics
longs for its lost China
Its lovely India Orquidia
(transfer from Granada to Manati
I saw Lorca there—holding the Sirens'
hands—her Boricua waist—a sunset
of alphabets)

In the childhood of his theater
Andalusia was a stage,
he was a page
For the proverbs of his Nana's hands,
listen there are songs
Which put us to sleep,
we hear them again in Harlem
The deep song of 125th Street
its blue desert toward
The water of screaming curves,
crown for the king of Granada,
Crown for the king of Harlem,
your womb of children,
Giving birth in Fuentevaqueros.
Terror and gentleness
Scream and kiss
Fire and roses.

A farmer of color crops,
Borges baptized him a painter
drawing with his words
Line-circles, a nation.

An old man stares in
a baby's glance,
Antiquity of old stone,
he made cities of the occult
So visible
we walk within them
We dance within them,
and through them the
birds fly.
We burn within them our flesh,
he left plazas of desire
For our fertile eyes,
balconies for our drama.
The water and the fire,
the women and the men,
The pants and the skirt,
and the road that leads
To the river illuminated.

Juan Rulfo

The little house alone
toward the exit of the town—
Makes a sort of sound
it comes from its struggle
To hold itself up.
As if the wood was breathing,
a kind of echo,
No one is there
yet so many roads
Come to an end
at its door.
A man walks down the street,
just about a skeleton,
Eyes hungry of roaming
wolf.
There is a smell of corn
and old women's hands,
Along with a howling
tinted with floral water
And candle wax.
The other people were
all somewhere enclosed,
More semblance of shadows,
outlines in the miasmic realms
Along the margin of the river.
It was all a whirlpool
no one saw anyone else,
Some murmurs of language
enough to make a passage
Through the air of hazy
webs,
Each pitch a worse lament.
Yet the words rise
like love licking bones
In winter.
Strong odor of grass
which never dies,

Patriarchal menace
power blind the creatures,
A conquest each time,
A submission each question,
a dialogue of whips.
Every word the available air
in a planet where oxygen
Has been exiled.
Enough breath for the bones
to continue
past the house.
Why go there?
There is no one there
in the past,
Only voices are heard,
like calcium scraping
Off of bones,
Names which no longer
have faces,
The future frustrated
from so much past.

Sometimes on the crust
of the earth
There is only sound.

CAMARÓN DE LA ISLA

His voice is the waves of
the Mediterranean Sea
Whatever sailed:
Phoenician barks,
Greek and Indian gestures
Moorish vapors out of his pores,
Arabian carabelas
into the deep rivers
Brahmin chains glittering
in cathedrals,
In his song the horses
which dashed out of the sea,
He sang to the moon of Sarah
which is always full,
Caravans like trails of ants
move through eons,
Something there invisible
he documented where history
hides.

The truth is always present
in obscurity,
Best for idiots not to sea
vessels disappearing beyond
The pillars of Hercules,
from the circle of those lost
to the archives but not
From the earth that sways them,
we hear a murmur arise,
A duende of light arrives
with the dawn
Over the snow cape Sierra Nevada
voices vortex into bellies,
Through the Albaicín
songs which have become streets
Leading toward Sacro Monte
where the blood lives inside rocks.

In Granada in a bar,
a gold watch reflects the moon,
And the eyes suddenly of a woman
as a favor from God,
All stationed in the shaking of
his voice,
which makes transparent cities
With hands like mist,
the walls and facades,
Covering the other gaiety
dripping with sadness,
A tragic perfume of enjoyment,
all the cities, all the nations,
All the borders,
we merely walk through the earth's
doors singing,
Camarón de la Isla brings
a voltage from paradise,
In this moment, in that moment,
which century,
His mouth the exit of an
active volcano,
As he stands like an open knife,
disfiguring the air.

JACK KEROUAC

There is always a time to eat the streets
when sounds and shapes are such voluptuous food.

A rhythm becomes a word
a movement becomes as it flies past
The engine which is painting it.

Americano writer
in the midst of music
The Lower East Side sector of
old brick walls—
California of lazy thought,
so afternoons Jack Daniels
Buddha stares rider-types
the countryside in his
Pocket like cherries.
Back east building boxes
Lit marijuana reefa,
scratchy victrola where
The harbinger nods taps
into the rural flow
Into the lines of the city.

A priest of certain words
candles lit—
Aware that they belong to you,
like Monk's piano which
Has his eyes staring through
the cymbals and horns,
There are immense things which
are truly ours
Like the things we see.
perceive how the night
of our initiations
Empires into experience.

Cityscape Manhattan skyline
listen how an old typewriter
Keeps Max Roach's beat,
strangers in the night
Become saxophone solos,
their features melting
Under rubber wheels.
In Kerouac's pages
speed tornado vertical
Metropolis animated
Walt Disney figures,
windows of swivel,
Paragraphs of mambo pirouette
Episodes just take off in flight,
Siiiiiiissssh
A gasping to reach the
actual speed real speed
Of the reel-
           Road Runner
devouring road tar
Flashing *On the Road*
To a sky of star desires,
to feel we want more
Beyond the boundaries of our flesh,
we become words that have
Come to the end of the road
turning around to eat themselves.

BEEP-BEEP

Moroccan Children

From the train through the window,
seeing how children break out running
near them shepherd parents—women squatted
into the soil—inside older sisters of
henna hands dream of love castles
the children fly like the wind
their hands raised
fists above heads
white shirts flapping like dove
wings.

Marrakesh umbral of the Sahara
spreads like carpet below the steel
of the locomotive
opens and you start to see the grains
of sand
small hands clutching how many pebbles?

The Medina like a circus
the streets like the snail's shell
Men eating fire
snakes rising from rugs
women diviners.

In the outskirts children
find each other and run
through the periphery of
the festival—that is every night
La'uds round belly sculptures
its strings of camel hair
plucking.

The children frolic and play tag
exhange fingers
then swift back to the skirts
of their mothers—

They seem like they would fall
at the corners of certain edges
but they miss all harm
all points are evaded.
Timing is their happiness—
verses repeat through their flesh
keeping them in safe flight.
They swirl out of turbans
from between women's jellabas,
prancing through sweet almond
fragrance,
Are they nuggets
or sweetened churros
small brown legs dancing
skidding through the Medina
plaza pavement,
elevating momentarily into the
air,
olive eyes full of the jinns
of joy
like children's book of
red balloons,
helium bubbles
a yellow globe escapes
only the children see
it rising toward the clouds,
only the children see the phenomenon,
see things the world drops,
forgotten gestures no one
pays mind to.
They collect memories of
oblivious seconds rolled into
cookies of nirvana dreams,
unknowing they look at awareness.

In their tongues
the sweet rhymes of glazed cakes
brown hazelnut powdered sugar,
sounds they swallow and taste
from tongue to toes,

forehead sparks and hair grows
in front of one while looking
at the rhythms of the dar drum
street musicians singers improvise
within a circle with a steel drum
upon the ground,
the drummers play it with their
feet
talk to each other
advance through violins
and accordions,
smells to me like other plazas
I have seen—
the whole Atlantean link flows,
the clapping the dar plenas
panderetas resound,
the tribes hidden from the
global investors,
obscuring invisible like
maraca seeds
becoming sound to censors
who scratch their heads.

The night envelops,
children walk away in
family balls
jaggedy of merriment
wobbling like the earth's
spin upon the axes,
they stare eye to eye,
speaking with the air,
they make you a circle,
or an oval like a date.

Voices blanket the dark
air
oozing from the honeycomb
balconies
through the streets of black
serene

veiled women pass
their eyes could produce
desert storms
or break marble statues
in two,
they whisk by like black
blankets flapping
clutching their children,
vanishing with a sort of laughter
sons and daughters
into the night of the desert.

They leave a flavor
of so much parchment
of so much skin of words.
I remain with my own childish
hands
tones that become moisture.
Later all gather around
a table,
the night the impact of
cool colors from the
open infinity of the
Sahara
their little fingers
reaching into the collective
large cous-cous dish,
the women make balls of
the food and push them
into their mouths.

Finally their young bodies
thrown about upon rugs
moving from dream to dream.

I repose upon a red sofa
it is my bed
through the window
some distant singing,
shadows are the syllables.

A lingering child comes
into the room
and gives me a hug
says something
I could only understand
with my bones.

Darker nocturn
I dream with delicate
Taino sculptures
made of seashells—
I am looking over a man
who chisels a mandala
upon a copper disc,
I am in this bohío,
I hear sound in Arawak,
the man is speaking Arabic
reading from a book,
I make it out as Spanish
print upon his forehead:
"El hogar de uno es donde hay
amor"

In the morning the scent of
mint,
a warm arabic voice kisses
verses.
The children were already
out playing
The cantico of their games,
rising once again,
in this place,
in such place.
                    —Marrakesh

Title Index

Colophon

Maraca was designed at Coffee House Press
in the Warehouse District of downtown Minneapolis.
The text is set in Perpetua with chapter headings in Shuriken Boy

The coffee house of seventeenth-century England was a place of fellowship where ideas could be freely exchanged. The coffee house of 1950s America was a place of refuge and of tremendous literary energy. At the turn of our latest century, coffee house culture abounds at corner shops and on-line. We hope this spirit welcomes our readers into the pages of Coffee House Press books.

Poetry Titles from Coffee House Press

Good books are brewing at coffeehousepress.org

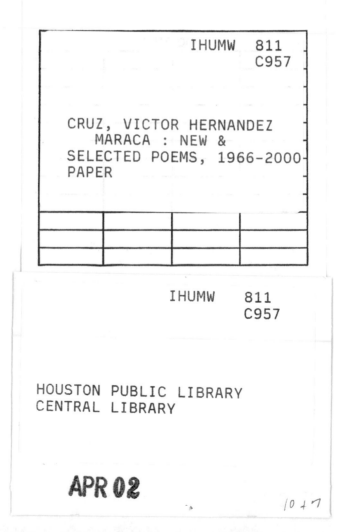